S0-ARJ-833

Table of Contents

*PLEASE NOTE: Page 52 (Spelling) includes a list of 100 words that students should learn to spell. These are high-frequency words that are often misspelled. This list may be given to determine proficiency at the beginning of the year. A copy could be sent home for students to use as homework over an extended period of time.

Class Record Chart

Students	Reading: Overall	Consonant Blends	Vowel Sounds	Word Meaning	Word Meaning in Context	Words with Multiple Meanings	Antonyms	Synonyms	Word Origin and Synonyms	Analogies	Affixes and Compound Words	Facts	Sequence	Context	Main Idea	Conclusion	Inference	Fantasy	Realistic Fiction	Nonfiction	Language Arts: Overall	Capitalization	Punctuation	Capitalization and Punctuation	Nouns	Verbs	Pronouns	Using Words Correctly	Sentence Parts	Clear Sentences
_____																														
_____																														
_____																														
_____																														
_____																														
_____																														
_____																														
_____																														
_____																														
_____																														
_____																														
_____																														
_____																														
_____																														
_____																														
_____																														
_____																														
_____																														
_____																														
_____																														
_____																														
_____																														
_____																														
_____																														

Class Record Chart

Students	Spelling	Reference Materials	Parts of a Book	Alphabetical Order	Charts and Graphs	Personal Narrative	Information Paragraph	How-To Paragraph	Persuasive Paragraph	**Math: Overall**	Number Concepts	Addition and Subtraction	Multiplication and Division	Mixed Operations	Geometry	Measurement	Fractions and Decimals	Statistics and Probability	Pre-Algebra: Patterns	Money	Time	Estimation	Problem Solving: Whole Numbers	Problem Solving: Measurement and Geometry	Problem Solving: Fractions and Decimals	**Science: Overall**	Earth and Space Science	Life Science	Physical Science	**Social Studies: Overall**	Reading Maps	Reading Time Lines

Class Record Chart

Assessments to Identify Skills and Needs 4, SV 3395-2

Name _____   Date _____

Individual Student Chart

	Test	Retest		Test	Retest
Reading: Overall			Reference Materials		
Consonant Blends			Parts of a Book		
Vowel Sounds			Alphabetical Order and Dictionary Skills		
Word Meaning			Charts and Graphs		
Word Meaning in Context			Personal Narrative		
Words with Multiple Meanings			Information Paragraph		
Antonyms			How-To Paragraph		
Synonyms			Persuasive Paragraph		
Word Origin and Synonyms			**Math: Overall**		
Analogies			Number Concepts		
Affixes and Compound Words			Addition and Subtraction		
Facts			Multiplication and Division		
Sequence			Mixed Operations with Whole Numbers		
Context			Geometry		
Main Idea			Measurement		
Conclusion			Fractions and Decimals		
Inference			Statistics and Probability		
Fantasy			Pre-Algebra: Patterns		
Realistic Fiction			Money		
Nonfiction			Time		
Language Arts: Overall			Estimation		
Capitalization			Problem Solving: Whole Numbers		
Punctuation			Problem Solving: Measurement and Geometry		
Capitalization and Punctuation			Problem Solving: Fractions and Decimals		
Nouns			**Science: Overall**		
Verbs			Earth and Space Science		
Pronouns			Life Science		
Using Words Correctly			Physical Science		
Sentence Parts			**Social Studies: Overall**		
Clear Sentences			Reading Maps		
Spelling			Reading Time Lines		

www.svschoolsupply.com

© Steck-Vaughn Company

Individual Student Chart

Assessments to Identify Skills and Needs 4, SV 3395-2

Reading Overall Assessment

Directions Darken the circle for the correct answer.

1. Some people like to ____ about their good grades.

   Ⓐ drag   Ⓑ shag   Ⓒ brag   Ⓓ None of these

2. The acrobat did an amazing ____ on the high wire.

   Ⓐ shunt   Ⓑ stunt   Ⓒ blunt   Ⓓ None of these

3. Birds are to feathers as fish are to ____.

   Ⓐ scales   Ⓑ rivers   Ⓒ trees   Ⓓ gills

4. Barge is to boat as taxi is to ____.

   Ⓐ bike   Ⓑ train   Ⓒ car   Ⓓ bus

5. Which word probably comes from the Old French word *colpon*, meaning "a piece cut off"?

   Ⓐ cotton   Ⓑ coupon   Ⓒ cushion   Ⓓ counting

Directions Darken the circle by the word that means the opposite of the underlined word.

6. My cousins arrived by train today.

   Ⓐ departed   Ⓑ moved   Ⓒ journeyed   Ⓓ came

7. She had to reject their generous offer.

   Ⓐ consider   Ⓑ refuse   Ⓒ accept   Ⓓ adjust

Directions Darken the circle by the word that has both underlined meanings.

8. it's found in your shoe or you have one in your mouth

   Ⓐ lace   Ⓑ tooth   Ⓒ tongue   Ⓓ heel

9. place for keeping money or side of a river

   Ⓐ safe   Ⓑ bank   Ⓒ stream   Ⓓ bridge

Go on to the next page.

Reading Overall Assessment, p. 2

(**Directions**) Darken the circle for the correct answer.

10. In 1888 there was a terrible **blizzard** in New York City. It lasted for three days. There were strong winds. Blowing snow was all that could be seen. Many people died in this storm.

In this paragraph, the word **blizzard** means

Ⓐ house   Ⓑ rain   Ⓒ guard   Ⓓ snowstorm

11. Some high school students have after-school jobs. Many states allow students to get working papers after they turn 14. There are rules about the kind of work students can do. They cannot work at dangerous jobs. There are rules about the number of hours and the times of day students can work.

Which of these would be the best title for the paragraph?

Ⓐ Why Students Work After School   Ⓒ Rules for Working After School

Ⓑ Getting a Good Job   Ⓓ How to Get Working Papers

12. It was a cold day, and Ali stared at the white snow that covered the sidewalk. He knew he had a lot of shoveling to do. He was supposed to clean off the whole sidewalk. Out in the street, Ali's friends were pulling their sleds. Ali knew they were going to have fun sledding down the hill. They called for him to come, but Ali just waved. As they walked away, Ali slowly started to shovel.

Which of these sentences is probably true?

Ⓐ Ali would rather work than play.   Ⓒ Ali loved to shovel snow.

Ⓑ The other children didn't like Ali.   Ⓓ When Ali had a job to do, he did it.

13. The President was coming to visit the small town. Everyone was very excited. All the people worked hard to clean up their town. They mowed the grass and swept the sidewalks. They fixed up the old houses. They even painted the water tower.

Which of these sentences is probably true?

Ⓐ The President was moving to the town.

Ⓑ The people were trying to fool the President.

Ⓒ The President only liked big towns.

Ⓓ The people wanted their town to look nice.

Consonant Blends

Directions Read each sentence below. Darken the circle next to the word that completes the sentence.

1. When people are sad, they may ____.

   Ⓐ fry   Ⓑ cry   Ⓒ try   Ⓓ dry

2. That mountain looks easy to ____.

   Ⓐ crime   Ⓑ slime   Ⓒ grime   Ⓓ climb

3. Weigh the grapes on the ____.

   Ⓐ shale   Ⓑ stale   Ⓒ scale   Ⓓ sale

4. Our teacher told us to turn the ____.

   Ⓐ page   Ⓑ sage   Ⓒ wage   Ⓓ cage

5. He used a microscope to study the ____.

   Ⓐ bell   Ⓑ sell   Ⓒ cell   Ⓓ tell

6. I want a cold ____.

   Ⓐ slink   Ⓑ drink   Ⓒ think   Ⓓ wink

7. Rain helps flowers to ____.

   Ⓐ know   Ⓑ slow   Ⓒ snow   Ⓓ grow

8. The sun shines during the ____.

   Ⓐ may   Ⓑ say   Ⓒ pay   Ⓓ day

9. The season after summer is ____.

   Ⓐ ball   Ⓑ fall   Ⓒ hall   Ⓓ call

10. Please hold your hands at your ____.

    Ⓐ tide   Ⓑ side   Ⓒ wide   Ⓓ hide

Name _____ Date _____

Vowel Sounds

Directions Read each sentence. Darken the circle next to the word that answers the question.

1. Which word has the same vowel sound as **fault**?

Ⓐ halt   Ⓑ cult   Ⓒ full

2. Which word starts with the **w** sound?

Ⓐ only   Ⓑ once   Ⓒ on

3. Which word sounds exactly like **meat**?

Ⓐ mite   Ⓑ mane   Ⓒ meet

4. Which word rhymes with **coal**?

Ⓐ cool   Ⓑ pole   Ⓒ coil

5. Which word has the same vowel sound as **joy**?

Ⓐ coin   Ⓑ loan   Ⓒ loon

6. Which means "to pull something"?

Ⓐ haul   Ⓑ hall   Ⓒ hull

7. Which word has the same vowel sound as **flour**?

Ⓐ pour   Ⓑ power   Ⓒ bought

8. Which is the opposite of **sour**?

Ⓐ swede   Ⓑ sweat   Ⓒ sweet

9. What is another name for **woman**?

Ⓐ lad   Ⓑ lady   Ⓒ laddie

10. Which is the number after **eight**?

Ⓐ nine   Ⓑ nun   Ⓒ None of these

Vowel Sounds

Directions Look at the underlined vowels in the first word of each row. Find the other word in the row that has the same vowel sound. Darken the circle next to the word that has the same vowel sound.

1. w<u>ai</u>t   Ⓐ maybe   Ⓑ again   Ⓒ time   Ⓓ said

2. h<u>ea</u>d   Ⓐ heed   Ⓑ fed   Ⓒ each   Ⓓ team

3. ab<u>ou</u>t   Ⓐ bought   Ⓑ score   Ⓒ hound   Ⓓ foot

4. <u>ar</u>t   Ⓐ sport   Ⓑ start   Ⓒ alert   Ⓓ turtle

5. wr<u>i</u>st   Ⓐ while   Ⓑ bird   Ⓒ limp   Ⓓ find

6. b<u>ou</u>ght   Ⓐ count   Ⓑ coat   Ⓒ though   Ⓓ daughter

7. f<u>ate</u>   Ⓐ weigh   Ⓑ father   Ⓒ thank   Ⓓ ball

8. l<u>aw</u>n   Ⓐ laugh   Ⓑ sauce   Ⓒ bale   Ⓓ sown

9. gr<u>ay</u>   Ⓐ all   Ⓑ salt   Ⓒ lazy   Ⓓ yawn

10. <u>air</u>   Ⓐ pear   Ⓑ rain   Ⓒ fire   Ⓓ four

11. l<u>u</u>nch   Ⓐ cute   Ⓑ luck   Ⓒ put   Ⓓ tune

12. th<u>ir</u>d   Ⓐ storm   Ⓑ hurt   Ⓒ hard   Ⓓ wire

13. st<u>o</u>ne   Ⓐ road   Ⓑ odd   Ⓒ look   Ⓓ pot

14. cr<u>y</u>   Ⓐ crib   Ⓑ puppy   Ⓒ first   Ⓓ sign

15. sh<u>ee</u>p   Ⓐ chew   Ⓑ eight   Ⓒ leak   Ⓓ fern

Word Meaning

Directions Read each meaning. Darken the circle next to the word that fits the meaning.

1. to go down

- Ⓐ achieve
- Ⓑ defense
- Ⓒ descend

2. not allowing water to enter

- Ⓐ water power
- Ⓑ watery
- Ⓒ waterproof

3. a tool that shows direction

- Ⓐ calculator
- Ⓑ compass
- Ⓒ computer

4. harm, or an illness

- Ⓐ mission
- Ⓑ sanitation
- Ⓒ infection

5. vitamins and minerals

- Ⓐ nutrients
- Ⓑ resources
- Ⓒ supplies

6. to annoy, or bother

- Ⓐ distract
- Ⓑ disgust
- Ⓒ compete

7. to make better

- Ⓐ interrupt
- Ⓑ interlace
- Ⓒ improve

8. a pledge or promise to keep

- Ⓐ commitment
- Ⓑ routine
- Ⓒ canopy

9. good or hopeful

- Ⓐ positive
- Ⓑ favorite
- Ⓒ popular

10. the idea or concept

- Ⓐ assignment
- Ⓑ principle
- Ⓒ object

11. a job or purpose

- Ⓐ cartographer
- Ⓑ experience
- Ⓒ function

12. to enter, or attack

- Ⓐ inflate
- Ⓑ identify
- Ⓒ invade

13. not open to harm

- Ⓐ submersible
- Ⓑ impossible
- Ⓒ immune

14. to want very much

- Ⓐ concentrate
- Ⓑ context
- Ⓒ crave

Word Meaning in Context

Directions Darken the circle for the word that fits in the blank.

1. Because of their humps, camels don't need much food when they travel across the desert. They don't ____ much water, either.

- (A) chew
- (B) require
- (C) fill
- (D) love

2. Camels sweat very little, so they don't use up the water in their ____.

- (A) bodies
- (B) hands
- (C) boxes
- (D) eyelashes

3. At the end of the year, all of the winners were ____ at a large banquet.

- (A) stung
- (B) honored
- (C) clapped
- (D) stolen

4. We were ____ by the strange noises we heard.

- (A) startled
- (B) served
- (C) strained
- (D) skilled

5. My father made a ____ for a room at a motel.

- (A) splash
- (B) dinner
- (C) sensation
- (D) reservation

6. We were all asked to ____ clothing for the flood victims.

- (A) wear
- (B) donate
- (C) frame
- (D) cool

7. Sal was asked to ____ the school band at the concert.

- (A) calm
- (B) close
- (C) carry
- (D) conduct

8. My mother ____ the juice concentrate.

- (A) sang
- (B) diluted
- (C) broke
- (D) drove

9. Native Americans thought that buffaloes were very ____ animals. The meat was used for food, and the hides were used for clothing and tents.

- (A) large
- (B) strange
- (C) useful
- (D) wild

10. Most people in China do not own cars. They use ____ instead.

- (A) sleds
- (B) bicycles
- (C) tools
- (D) magazines

11. Many people enjoy going to ____ to see the art exhibits.

- (A) movies
- (B) stores
- (C) theaters
- (D) museums

12. The team played in the softball ____.

- (A) tournament
- (B) race
- (C) pool
- (D) recreation

Words with Multiple Meanings

Directions Darken the circle by the word that fits both sentences.

1. This is the most ____ route to the cabin.
Could you ____ me to the library?
- Ⓐ direct
- Ⓑ scenic
- Ⓒ point
- Ⓓ difficult

2. Louisa will begin the first ____ tomorrow.
She will probably ____ all the papers tonight.
- Ⓐ lesson
- Ⓑ read
- Ⓒ finish
- Ⓓ grade

3. The doctor carefully weighed the baby on the ____.
He was able to ____ the garden wall easily.
- Ⓐ table
- Ⓑ scale
- Ⓒ climb
- Ⓓ repair

4. We had to ____ through the forest.
The blacksmith worked for hours over the hot ____.
- Ⓐ go
- Ⓑ furnace
- Ⓒ forge
- Ⓓ metal

5. Do you ____ the new tax plan?
Please do this ____ for me.
- Ⓐ like
- Ⓑ chore
- Ⓒ favor
- Ⓓ task

6. Please ____ the car in the driveway.
Yolanda went to the ____ to walk her dog.
- Ⓐ leave
- Ⓑ park
- Ⓒ trail
- Ⓓ country

7. There is no need to ____ your voice.
How much money did we ____ for the community shelter?
- Ⓐ collect
- Ⓑ spend
- Ⓒ raise
- Ⓓ lower

8. How did Bernard's sheep get out of their ____?
I need a ____ to fill out this form.
- Ⓐ pencil
- Ⓑ pen
- Ⓒ yard
- Ⓓ cage

9. Ahmad is learning the ancient ____ of weaving.
Small sailing ____ filled the harbor.
- Ⓐ art
- Ⓑ boats
- Ⓒ skill
- Ⓓ craft

10. Grandmother found an old ____ in the basement.
The elephant uses its ____ to drink water.
- Ⓐ bicycle
- Ⓑ mouth
- Ⓒ trunk
- Ⓓ desk

Antonyms

Directions Darken the circle for the word that means the <u>opposite</u> of the underlined word.

1. We all <u>chuckled</u> when a monkey did funny tricks.

   (A) roared   (C) smiled
   (B) laughed   (D) cried

2. Everyone was served a <u>generous</u> portion of pasta.

   (A) stingy   (C) large
   (B) huge   (D) full

3. Jerry sanded the wood to a <u>smooth</u> finish.

   (A) shiny   (C) rough
   (B) polished   (D) plain

4. I thought she received an <u>unjust</u> punishment.

   (A) wrong   (C) mean
   (B) fair   (D) terrible

5. Food was <u>scarce</u> on the long journey.

   (A) delicious (C) abundant
   (B) growing   (D) frozen

6. The old man grew very <u>feeble</u> after his illness.

   (A) weak   (C) strong
   (B) sad   (D) fragile

7. I think the hat he bought is <u>ugly</u>.

   (A) charming   (C) practical
   (B) beautiful (D) useful

8. The <u>giant</u> poodle would not stop barking.

   (A) miniature (C) black
   (B) loud   (D) old

9. She wore <u>sturdy</u> shoes on the mountain hike.

   (A) flimsy   (C) comfortable
   (B) leather   (D) heavy

10. Should we <u>extend</u> our vacation by one week?

   (A) lengthen   (C) shorten
   (B) continue   (D) enjoy

Synonyms

Directions Darken the word that means the <u>same</u> or <u>almost the same</u> as the underlined word.

1. Be sure to <u>conceal</u> the surprise gift.
   - Ⓐ hide
   - Ⓑ wrap
   - Ⓒ buy
   - Ⓓ order

2. That is an <u>obsolete</u> tool.
   - Ⓐ old
   - Ⓑ fancy
   - Ⓒ different
   - Ⓓ strange

3. I see a very <u>rapid</u> river current.
   - Ⓐ strong
   - Ⓑ weak
   - Ⓒ swift
   - Ⓓ slow

4. We heard a <u>thunderous</u> sound.
   - Ⓐ whispery
   - Ⓑ strange
   - Ⓒ musical
   - Ⓓ noisy

5. I saw a <u>fabulous</u> movie last week.
   - Ⓐ silly
   - Ⓑ funny
   - Ⓒ great
   - Ⓓ lovely

6. There was a <u>heap</u> of books on the floor.
   - Ⓐ pile
   - Ⓑ box
   - Ⓒ bag
   - Ⓓ number

7. They tried to <u>block</u> cars from using the road.
   - Ⓐ stop
   - Ⓑ swing
   - Ⓒ fix
   - Ⓓ pave

8. You need to <u>enlarge</u> this picture to see the details.
   - Ⓐ print
   - Ⓑ magnify
   - Ⓒ block
   - Ⓓ trim

9. Most people use a <u>remote</u> control to turn on their TV set.
   - Ⓐ handy
   - Ⓑ rough
   - Ⓒ nearby
   - Ⓓ distant

10. Ernie felt <u>drowsy</u> after sitting through a long movie.
    - Ⓐ hungry
    - Ⓑ sleepy
    - Ⓒ thirsty
    - Ⓓ sloppy

Word Origin and Synonyms

Directions

Darken the circle for the modern word that most likely comes from the original word.

1. Which word probably comes from the Middle English *poselen*, meaning "confuse" or "bewilder"?

   Ⓐ puzzle   Ⓒ posse
   Ⓑ push   Ⓓ pester

2. Which word probably comes from the Latin *luna*, meaning "moonstruck"?

   Ⓐ loop   Ⓒ long
   Ⓑ lunatic   Ⓓ loose

3. Which word probably comes from the Greek *bi kyklos*, meaning "two circles"?

   Ⓐ binder   Ⓒ bifocal
   Ⓑ bicycle   Ⓓ billion

4. Which word probably comes from the Arabic *makhazin*, meaning "storehouse"?

   Ⓐ magnet   Ⓒ magazine
   Ⓑ margarine Ⓓ margin

5. Which word probably comes from the Spanish *hamaca*, meaning "a kind of cloth swing"?

   Ⓐ hamper   Ⓒ hammer
   Ⓑ ham   Ⓓ hammock

Directions

Darken the circle for the word that means the <u>same</u> or <u>almost the same</u> as the underlined word.

6. <u>swing</u> back and forth

   Ⓐ break   Ⓒ skip
   Ⓑ sway   Ⓓ jump

7. in a good <u>mood</u>

   Ⓐ idea   Ⓒ state of mind
   Ⓑ play   Ⓓ way to go

8. great <u>pleasure</u>

   Ⓐ fear   Ⓒ worry
   Ⓑ satisfaction Ⓓ dislike

9. <u>practice</u> for the play

   Ⓐ study   Ⓒ sing
   Ⓑ call   Ⓓ rehearse

10. the baby <u>crept</u>

    Ⓐ fell   Ⓒ slept
    Ⓑ crawled   Ⓓ stood

Analogies

Directions Think about how the first two words are related. Darken the circle next to the word that best completes the analogy.

1. Crown is to frown as fling is to ___.

Ⓐ brown   Ⓒ toss

Ⓑ throw   Ⓓ bring

2. Clean is to dirty as top is to ___.

Ⓐ soap   Ⓒ tree

Ⓑ bottom   Ⓓ head

3. Run is to track as swim is to ___.

Ⓐ dive   Ⓒ pool

Ⓑ wet   Ⓓ winter

4. Shiny is to dull as happy is to ___.

Ⓐ glad   Ⓒ bright

Ⓑ funny   Ⓓ sad

5. Carrot is to beet as pencil is to ___.

Ⓐ paper   Ⓒ eraser

Ⓑ pen   Ⓓ lead

6. Fingers are to hands as toes are to ___.

Ⓐ shoes   Ⓒ gloves

Ⓑ feet   Ⓓ thumbs

7. Glad is to bad as big is to ___.

Ⓐ pig   Ⓒ small

Ⓑ had   Ⓓ large

8. Road is to car as track is to ___.

Ⓐ truck   Ⓒ plane

Ⓑ bus   Ⓓ train

9. Pull is to push as sit is to ___.

Ⓐ walk   Ⓒ hop

Ⓑ stand   Ⓓ tug

10. Broom is to sweep as shovel is to ___.

Ⓐ mess   Ⓒ hole

Ⓑ dig   Ⓓ hoe

Affixes and Compound Words

Directions
Darken the circle for the word that has a prefix or suffix.

1. Ⓐ complete
   Ⓑ honor
   Ⓒ happy
   Ⓓ improper

2. Ⓐ disappear
   Ⓑ sanitary
   Ⓒ believe
   Ⓓ mobile

3. Ⓐ polite
   Ⓑ courageous
   Ⓒ dress
   Ⓓ real

4. Ⓐ amusement
   Ⓑ possible
   Ⓒ common
   Ⓓ patient

5. Ⓐ publish
   Ⓑ sincerely
   Ⓒ invent
   Ⓓ advise

Directions
Darken the circle for the compound word.

6. Ⓐ unhappy
   Ⓑ nonpayment
   Ⓒ bumpier
   Ⓓ proofread

7. Ⓐ confession
   Ⓑ company
   Ⓒ raindrops
   Ⓓ proclamation

8. Ⓐ excellent
   Ⓑ football
   Ⓒ auditorium
   Ⓓ nonskid

9. Ⓐ secretly
   Ⓑ sunshine
   Ⓒ babyish
   Ⓓ finished

10. Ⓐ uncomfortable
    Ⓑ planning
    Ⓒ trainer
    Ⓓ downtown

Facts

Directions Read the story. Then read each sentence below. Darken the circle for the answer that best completes the sentence.

There's nothing really new about beards. Men have been growing beards for thousands of years. If a man does not shave his chin and the sides of his face, a beard will grow. Long ago almost all men had beards.

The first men to shave off their beards were the early Egyptians. But not all Egyptian men shaved. Some spent hours caring for their beards. They dyed them, braided them, and even wove gold threads into them. The kings and queens of Egypt sometimes wore false beards called postiches. A postiche was a sign of royalty. It was made of metal and attached to the chin with straps of gold.

Some men in ancient Greece wore beards. They thought a beard was a sign of wisdom. Socrates was a famous Greek who wore a beard. He was also thought to be a wise man.

1. Long ago almost all men had ____.

Ⓐ postiches
Ⓑ beards
Ⓒ gold
Ⓓ wisdom

2. The kings of Egypt sometimes wore ____.

Ⓐ false beards
Ⓑ wise beards
Ⓒ diamond beards
Ⓓ cloth beards

3. If a man doesn't shave, he will grow a ____.

Ⓐ nose
Ⓑ beard
Ⓒ braid
Ⓓ chin

4. A postiche was a sign of ____.

Ⓐ weakness
Ⓑ loyalty
Ⓒ royalty
Ⓓ marriage

5. A famous Greek who wore a beard was ____.

Ⓐ Postiche
Ⓑ Burnside
Ⓒ Egyptian
Ⓓ Socrates

6. The first men to shave off their beards were the ____.

Ⓐ Greeks
Ⓑ English
Ⓒ wise men
Ⓓ Egyptians

Sequence

Directions

Darken the circle by the sentence that should come <u>first</u>.

1. Ⓐ Then, she climbed into the canoe.
   Ⓑ Erin always put on her life jacket before she would go canoeing.
   Ⓒ Next, she untied it from the dock and got her paddle in hand.
   Ⓓ Finally, she headed out onto the lake.

2. Ⓐ The Siberian tiger spends much of its time hunting.
   Ⓑ The tiger drags the prey to cover, eats its fill, and covers the remains to eat later after resting.
   Ⓒ Then, the tiger pounces and grabs the prey by the back of the neck, killing it.
   Ⓓ First, it creeps to within 30 to 80 feet of its prey.

3. Ⓐ It's possible that millions of years ago, a huge meteorite hit Earth and caused dinosaurs to become extinct.
   Ⓑ Since plant-eating dinosaurs had no food, they all died.
   Ⓒ With no sunlight, all the plants died.
   Ⓓ After the meteorite hit, it caused a huge cloud of dust to shut out sunlight.

Directions

Darken the circle by the sentence that should come <u>last</u>.

4. Ⓐ The audience jumps to its feet and applauds the beautiful performance.
   Ⓑ The music begins quietly, growing louder.
   Ⓒ Dancers leap across the stage.
   Ⓓ As the music ends, the dancers slowly leave the stage.

5. Ⓐ The first sign of spring is often buds on a tree.
   Ⓑ Soon, green leaves emerge.
   Ⓒ Day by day, the buds open into flowers.
   Ⓓ When summer arrives, the tree is covered in leaves.

6. Ⓐ All day the octopus stays hidden in its nest.
   Ⓑ The octopus digs a gravel nest.
   Ⓒ Then, at night, it comes out to hunt, changing color to blend in with its surroundings.
   Ⓓ The octopus hunts by grabbing a crab, crayfish, or mollusk with its long arms, using suckers to grip its slippery prey.

Context

(**Directions**) Darken the circle for the correct answer.

1. Pluto is the planet farthest from the sun. Not much is known about that **distant** planet. It is quite cold there since it is so far from the sun. Scientists don't think that there is any life on Pluto.

    In this paragraph, the word **distant** means

    Ⓐ faraway   Ⓒ lucky
    Ⓑ nearby   Ⓓ pleasant

2. Piranhas are fish. They live in South American rivers. These fish tend to swim in large groups. They will tear the flesh off an animal or person that gets in the water. In just minutes all that is left is the **skeleton**.

    In this paragraph, the word **skeleton** means

    Ⓐ key   Ⓒ butter
    Ⓑ pie   Ⓓ bones

3. The skunk has a special way to protect itself. It sprays its enemies with a liquid from under its tail. This liquid has a **foul** smell. So the skunk is left alone.

    In this paragraph, the word **foul** means

    Ⓐ great   Ⓒ cloudy
    Ⓑ dandy   Ⓓ terrible

4. The roadrunner is a bird. It is one of the fastest hunters in the desert. It can run up to twenty miles an hour. It moves so fast that it can kill a snake. The roadrunner's long legs also help it **flee** from its enemies.

    In this paragraph, the word **flee** means

    Ⓐ want   Ⓒ run
    Ⓑ know   Ⓓ set

5. The leek is a plant like the onion. The people of Wales **respect** the leek. Long ago it helped them fight a war. They could not tell who was on their side. So the people from Wales put leeks in their caps.

    In this paragraph, the word **respect** means

    Ⓐ like   Ⓒ build
    Ⓑ melt   Ⓓ turn

Main Idea

Directions Darken the circle by the title that tells the main idea of each paragraph.

1. When the Revolutionary War began, the American colonies stopped using the English flag. Each of the thirteen colonies used a different flag. This was so confusing that George Washington wrote to Congress and said, "Please fix some flag by which our vessels will know each other."

Ⓐ Why the Colonies Needed One Flag
Ⓑ Flags of the Thirteen Colonies
Ⓒ How We Won the Revolutionary War
Ⓓ Using the English Flag

2. On September 16, 1620, a group of 100 men, women, and children left England on a ship called the *Mayflower*. The trip would take them across the Atlantic Ocean to make new homes in Virginia. Their three-month journey was difficult. They finally reached dry land at Plymouth Rock, Massachusetts, on December 26. The weary travelers decided against going on to Virginia, and settled in Massachusetts.

Ⓐ A Ship Called the *Mayflower*
Ⓑ People of Plymouth Rock
Ⓒ New Homes in Virginia
Ⓓ A Long and Difficult Journey

3. A small lizard, called a gecko, has a special way of protecting itself. When attacked, it simply drops off its tail. The tail keeps wriggling on the ground, confusing attackers. Soon new cells will grow where the tail dropped off. This growth is called a bud. After about eight to twelve months, the gecko has a new, full-sized tail.

Ⓐ A Wriggling Tail
Ⓑ How Geckos Protect Themselves
Ⓒ Growing a New Tail
Ⓓ From Cells to Buds

4. Several years ago a horse named Charon won six races. He earned $93,000. Charon won the races because he is afraid of other horses. When Charon sees horses near him, he tries to get away from them. He gets away by running fast and staying out front, often winning the race.

Ⓐ Winning Six Races
Ⓑ Why Charon Wins Races
Ⓒ Dean Watson's Horse
Ⓓ How to Win $93,000

Conclusion

Directions Read the story. Darken the circle for the phrase that best completes the sentence.

1. Most desert plants have sharp stickers. These spines help the desert plant drink water. Morning mist forms big drops on these stickers. Then the drops fall, and the plant drinks the water. The spines also make the hot desert winds circle around the plant. This keeps the wind from taking the plant's water.

   From this story you can tell that

   Ⓐ most desert plants need spines to live.
   Ⓑ the spines on desert plants do not help them.
   Ⓒ desert plants do not live very long.
   Ⓓ the wind does not blow in the desert.

2. The man tried to balance himself, but he wobbled. The wheels seemed to go in every direction at once. When he hit a bump, his foot lost its grip on the pedal. He put his feet on the ground. Then he let go of the handlebars and sat straight up on the narrow seat with his arms forward. "I haven't done this in a long time," he said with a laugh.

   You can tell that the man is

   Ⓐ driving a car for the first time in a long time.
   Ⓑ trying to use a mixer in the kitchen.
   Ⓒ trying to ride a tricycle.
   Ⓓ trying to ride a bicycle.

3. Jay and Jean went to the store to buy toys for their baby. "Let's get a toy cat that has painted eyes," said Jay. "Button eyes can fall off, and the baby might eat them." They also wanted a wooden train set. Jean made sure that the train didn't have any sharp edges. They also bought a set of paints. The paints were marked *Safe for all ages*. Jay and Jean knew that their baby would like these toys.

   From this story you can tell that

   Ⓐ Jean was a painting teacher.
   Ⓑ Jean liked the train set the best.
   Ⓒ Jean and Jay bought only safe toys.
   Ⓓ Jean wanted a train with sharp edges.

Inference

(**Directions**) Read the story. Darken the circle for the sentence that best answers the question.

1. The day was sunny and hot. Ava stood happily at the side of the swimming pool. She thought about the clear blue water. Then she jumped in. But as she began swimming, she started shaking, and her skin began to turn blue.

    Which of these sentences is probably true?

    (A) The water was very hot.   (C) The water was very cold.
    (B) Ava forgot to wear her coat.   (D) Ava didn't know how to swim.

2. Jan was always playing basketball. In fact, she almost never left the basketball court. Jan started practicing early every morning. As the sun went down, Jan was still bouncing the basketball.

    Which of these sentences is probably true?

    (A) Jan slept at the basketball court.
    (B) Tennis was very important to Jan.
    (C) Jan wanted to be a great basketball player.
    (D) The basketball was too big to bounce inside.

3. If you are sick and you cough or sneeze on someone, that person could get sick, too. But it is not really a good idea to stop yourself from sneezing. If you do, you could pull a muscle in your face. You could also make your nose bleed.

    Which of these sentences is probably true?

    (A) Sneezing makes your nose bleed.
    (B) Stopping a sneeze could be harmful.
    (C) You can get over a cold by not sneezing.
    (D) Sneezing is good exercise for your face.

4. One day Ann heard her friend Tom talking. Tom was telling everybody how smart his dog was. Tom said his dog could do tricks and could even ride a bicycle. But Ann knew that Tom's dog was just like any other dog. So Ann just smiled as Tom went on talking.

    Which of these sentences is probably true?

    (A) Ann didn't understand Tom's story.
    (B) Tom wanted to make Ann mad at him.
    (C) Ann didn't want to hurt Tom's feelings.
    (D) Tom had two dogs and a cat.

A Roman Myth

Many years ago, people who lived in Rome believed that gods and goddesses ruled the world. Jupiter was called the God of the Heavens, and Pluto was the God of the Underworld.

Ceres was the mother of all the Earth and the Goddess of All Growing Things. She lived with her daughter Prosperina in a valley. Everything was always sunny, blooming, and beautiful in that valley. One day Prosperina saw a plant that was very different from all the others. It was very tall and had more than one hundred blossoms on it.

Just as Prosperina tried to break off one of the blossoms, the ground began to rumble. Out of a great black hole sprang a golden chariot drawn by four black horses. A very angry-looking king sat in the chariot. Pluto reached out and pulled Prosperina into the chariot. Then they disappeared into the king's dark and dreary underground palace. Apollo, God of the Sun, saw what had happened. When Apollo told Ceres about her daughter, Ceres hid herself in dark places and cried and cried. She didn't care about any of the growing things in the valley anymore. Soon it looked as if all the living things on Earth would die. Jupiter pleaded with Ceres to take care of the Earth again, but she wouldn't listen. She wanted Prosperina to come back.

Jupiter sent Mercury, his swiftest messenger, to ask Pluto to release Prosperina. Pluto agreed to let her go, but before she left, he wanted her to eat something. He gave her a pomegranate.

When Prosperina returned to Earth, she told her mother all about her stay, even about eating the pomegranate. Ceres started to weep again. She believed that her daughter would have to return to the Underworld forever because she had tasted Pluto's food. Jupiter told Prosperina that she would have to spend a month in the Underworld for every seed she had eaten. Prosperina told her mother that she had only eaten four seeds, so she would only have to leave for four months.

Now every year when Prosperina returns to Pluto's palace, Ceres withdraws into the dark places and weeps for her daughter. All nature sleeps while Prosperina is away.

Go on to the next page.

A Roman Myth, p. 2

Directions Answer each question about the story. Darken the circle for the correct answer.

1. Another good title for this story could be ____.

   Ⓐ Pluto and His Chariot
   Ⓑ Ceres' Beautiful Valley
   Ⓒ Why Winter Lasts for Four Months
   Ⓓ Prosperina and Jupiter

2. This kind of story is called a ____.

   Ⓐ myth
   Ⓑ fable
   Ⓒ narrative
   Ⓓ poem

3. Why did Jupiter send Mercury to ask Pluto to return Prosperina?

   Ⓐ Mercury knew Pluto.
   Ⓑ Apollo said that Mercury should go to Pluto.
   Ⓒ Mercury was the fastest messenger.
   Ⓓ Mercury knew the way.

4. What season is it when Prosperina returns to Pluto's Underworld?

   Ⓐ winter
   Ⓑ spring
   Ⓒ summer
   Ⓓ fall

5. What does the word *pleaded* mean in this story?

   Ⓐ cried
   Ⓑ asked
   Ⓒ sent
   Ⓓ begged

6. How many months would Prosperina be able to stay with Ceres?

   Ⓐ 12 months
   Ⓑ 8 months
   Ⓒ 4 months
   Ⓓ 6 months

7. How did the Romans explain events that they didn't understand?

   Ⓐ They spoke to Jupiter.
   Ⓑ They told each other fables.
   Ⓒ They created myths about gods and goddesses.
   Ⓓ They prayed to Pluto.

8. Why did Pluto first take Prosperina underground?

   Ⓐ Prosperina tried to take a blossom from a special plant.
   Ⓑ Jupiter told him to take her.
   Ⓒ Ceres was crying.
   Ⓓ Mercury ate his pomegranate seeds.

Sylvia's Bear

Once there was a very rich girl who seemed to have everything she could ever want. She had closets full of clothes, most of which she never wore. She had an entire room just to hold all her toys, many of which she never played with. She had every new gadget that was advertised on television or radio for children. One might think that this girl might be spoiled and unpleasant, but she was very sweet and kind. She always shared whatever she had. She often gave things away, too. Her parents just couldn't resist buying her new things because they loved her and she was their only child.

One day the girl got a package in the mail. It contained a small stuffed bear. The bear was made of scraps of material of every color and pattern, and it was stitched together by hand. It had mismatched button eyes and a little green velvet vest. The note in its pocket said, "Thank You, to Sylvia from L." Sylvia was certain that this bear must be from Lin, a girl in her class at school. Sylvia had given Lin some clothes and toys for her family. She had never expected anything in return. She knew that Lin did not have money for presents. Lin had made this little bear to repay Sylvia's kindness.

It happened that shortly after Sylvia received the bear, there was a terrible fire at her house. Her family had to run out into the night as fire raged through their lovely home. Suddenly, Sylvia ran back into the house. Her parents screamed for her to stop. Soon, Sylvia ran back out the door, unharmed. Her parents demanded to know what she was thinking. They could replace anything she lost in the fire.

"You could not replace this," said Sylvia, holding out the little patched bear. Her parents shook their heads, mystified. But the truth was, the bear meant more to Sylvia than anything else she had ever owned.

Go on to the next page.

Sylvia's Bear, p. 2

Directions Answer the questions in complete sentences.

1. Why did Sylvia love the little bear more than anything else she owned?

_____

_____

_____

_____

2. Describe Sylvia.

_____

_____

_____

3. Why did Sylvia's parents tell her to stop as she ran back into the house?

_____

_____

_____

_____

4. Why did Lin give Sylvia the bear?

_____

_____

_____

5. Where did Sylvia find the bear?

_____

_____

_____

Memorial Day

Memorial Day was one of Junie's favorite holidays. She loved the parade and the ceremony in the town square. The band played taps and "The Star Spangled Banner." Now that she was older, she understood the ceremony better. She felt sad and grateful for the soldiers who had died. Afterward, Junie got to see all her relatives as they gathered at her house for a barbecue. She liked the way the holiday seemed to signal the beginning of summer. There were always a few weeks of school after Memorial Day, but they flew right by. Then it was vacation time!

This year, Junie was ten. The town parade did not seem as long or as grand as it had when she was younger, but she still liked it. As always, her grandparents, aunts, uncles, and cousins gathered at her parents' house. Everyone brought all kinds of salads, desserts, and other treats. Junie's Uncle Jess was there. He always brought a present for Junie and her brother, Adam. This was usually the only time of year they got to see him. He liked to make it more special. Last year, he had brought them a rubber raft for the stream. The year before they had gotten a tent for camping in the backyard. She couldn't wait to see what he would bring this year.

Junie, Adam, and their cousins played games of tag and baseball. They told each other stories about what had been going on in their lives since the last gathering. Then it was time to eat. Later, everyone had finished eating and was relaxing and talking. Uncle Jess looked at Junie and Adam. Junie and Adam looked at each other with barely concealed excitement. They followed their uncle to the back of his truck. When everyone saw Junie and Adam again, they were riding a tandem bicycle. It was the best present yet! Everyone took turns riding it up and down the long driveway for the rest of the afternoon. When the day was over, Junie and Adam rode down the drive with each car, waving and calling, "Good-bye!" until each one was out of sight.

Go on to the next page.

Memorial Day, p. 2

Directions Answer each question about the story. Darken the circle for the correct answer.

1. Junie and Adam probably live ____.

   Ⓐ in the city
   Ⓑ in an apartment
   Ⓒ in the country
   Ⓓ downtown

2. What is special about a *tandem* bicycle?

   Ⓐ Two people can ride it.
   Ⓑ It has four wheels.
   Ⓒ Three people can ride it.
   Ⓓ The pedals move by themselves.

3. What did Junie like about Memorial Day?

   Ⓐ She liked to be in the parade.
   Ⓑ She liked to see her relatives.
   Ⓒ She liked going to her uncle's house.
   Ⓓ She liked making the desserts.

4. Why did Uncle Jess bring a present for Junie and Adam?

   Ⓐ It was their birthday.
   Ⓑ They asked for one.
   Ⓒ Everyone brought presents.
   Ⓓ He didn't see them often.

5. What is the meaning of *concealed*?

   Ⓐ destroyed
   Ⓑ excited
   Ⓒ hidden
   Ⓓ found

Dream Team

John got the ball and drove it down the full length of the court. He knew he was handling the ball well. He reached the basket and put the ball up against the backboard. It went through the basket with a neat swoosh as John landed back on the court. A few of his Panther teammates clapped and John looked to his coach for approval, but Coach Penn was shaking his head. That was not the reaction John had expected. What was wrong?

"Everybody on the bleachers, now!" called the coach. When they had all found a seat, he studied them for a moment. "I see a good bunch of ball players here," said Coach Penn. "I also see a team that won't win a game if something doesn't change. Do you know what that is?" The boys were silent. "Teamwork!" said the coach, throwing his hands up in the air. "You have to start working together! John, you think you just made a great basket. Well, it went in the basket all right, but when you're playing a team sport, you need to act as a team. You support each other, and you use each other—pass the ball, look for the open man. No player on this team stands alone; you work together, or you don't play. Now let me see some teamwork!"

The boys got back on the court. They practiced working together and passing. They had to learn to trust each other and to be there for each other. John began to look at his teammates in a different way. He began to think of the team as parts of a machine that needed to work together. He still got to the hoop and made some shots, but he did it only when it was the team's best chance to get the points.

That Friday's competition was against the Bulldogs, who had beat John's team twice last year. This time, the Panthers played the best game they had played all season. They worked together on the court like the machine John had imagined earlier in the week. The crowd screamed and cheered. It was a close game, but when the final buzzer sounded, the Panthers had won, and every player had contributed to the victory. Coach Penn couldn't stop smiling. "Now that's the team I've been looking for!" he said.

Go on to the next page.

Dream Team, p. 2

Directions Answer each question with a complete sentence.

1. What is the meaning of *reaction*?

_____

_____

2. Why did Coach Penn shake his head at practice?

_____

_____

_____

3. What kind of team was the Panthers?

_____

_____

4. What team did the Panthers play on Friday?

_____

_____

5. Who contributed to the Panthers' victory?

_____

_____

No Lock Could Hold Him

The police officer walked into the locksmith's shop. He brought with him a handcuffed prisoner.

"The lock on these cuffs is broken," the police officer said. "I need you to cut the cuffs off."

Erich Weiss tried to cut the cuffs, but the steel was too hard. Weiss later said, "I broke six saw blades. Then a thought struck me. Maybe I could pick the lock."

Weiss succeeded. In fact, he picked the lock so easily that he soon tried others. Weiss used his new skill to put together a magic act. And he gave himself a new name—Harry Houdini.

Between 1895 and 1926, Houdini's act stunned the world. It seemed that he could escape from anything. He escaped from boxes, safes, and prison rooms.

In 1903, Houdini took his act to Russia. There he met Moscow's chief of police.

"Please lock me in your jail. I'd like to prove that I can escape from it," he said.

The chief had heard about Houdini's magic. He wanted no part in it. He turned Houdini down.

"How about the Carette, then?" Houdini asked.

The chief smiled. The Carette was a six-foot-square steel box. It was used to carry Russia's worst prisoners to Siberia. The Carette had two openings. One was a tiny window with bars. The other was a steel door. The chief could lock the door. But he could not unlock it. The key was 2,000 miles away in Siberia.

The chief made Houdini take off his clothes. He searched him for tools. He handcuffed Houdini and chained his legs together. Houdini got into the box, and the chief locked the door.

For the next 28 minutes, the chief waited. "He'll never get out," he thought.

Go on to the next page.

No Lock Could Hold Him, p. 2

But suddenly, Houdini appeared from behind the Carette. The door was still locked. The handcuffs and chains were also locked and lying on the floor. Somehow Houdini had escaped. No one ever found out how he did it.

Back in America, Houdini came up with another great act. A large glass box was placed on the stage. Houdini stood inside the box. A heavy piece of glass was lowered onto the box. The cover was locked on each side. Four tight straps passed over and under the box. Then water was poured into the box from a small hole in the top. Houdini was trapped. He had no way to reach the locks or straps. He had no way to breathe, either.

Houdini's helper pulled a curtain in front of the box. No one could breathe under water. In four or five minutes, he would drown. As the minutes passed, people began to panic. They feared Houdini was dead.

Then, suddenly, the curtain was pulled back. There stood Houdini, dripping wet. Behind him was the glass box. It was still filled with water. Its locks and straps were still in place. Houdini smiled at the people in the crowd. He had tricked them again.

Then Houdini came up with yet another trick. This time he climbed into a box that was bolted shut. The box was lowered six feet into the ground. The hole was filled with 3,000 pounds of sand.

The audience watched fearfully. Houdini was buried alive! He could never escape from the bolted box. And even if he did, he would be crushed by the heavy sand.

But all at once, the sand moved. A moment later, Houdini's curly head popped out. Once again the great Houdini had mysteriously escaped death.

Go on to the next page.

No Lock Could Hold Him, p. 3

Directions Darken the circle next to the answer that best completes the sentence.

1. When Houdini came out of the glass box, he was

 Ⓐ soaking wet.   Ⓑ coughing.   Ⓒ sick.

2. Houdini found it easy to

 Ⓐ write books.   Ⓑ bend coins.   Ⓒ pick locks.

3. Before opening his magic act, Houdini worked in a

 Ⓐ locksmith shop.   Ⓑ post office.   Ⓒ circus.

4. Houdini was the first person ever to escape from

 Ⓐ Russia.   Ⓑ the Carette.   Ⓒ jail.

Directions Darken the circle for the meaning that fits the word in **bold**.

5. People stared **fearfully** at the glass box.

 Ⓐ with great hope   Ⓑ with fear   Ⓒ secretly

6. The box was **bolted** before it was put in the ground.

 Ⓐ painted   Ⓑ opened   Ⓒ locked with a bar

7. The **audience** was afraid Houdini would drown.

 Ⓐ child   Ⓑ people watching   Ⓒ deaf person

8. Houdini **succeeded** in getting out of the Carette.

 Ⓐ was able to   Ⓑ feared   Ⓒ forgot

9. People were **stunned** by Houdini's act.

 Ⓐ angered   Ⓑ badly hurt   Ⓒ surprised

10. Houdini knew it was important not to **panic**.

 Ⓐ become frightened   Ⓑ cry   Ⓒ shout loudly

Circling the World

Ferdinand Magellan held his breath. He couldn't wait to hear what King Charles V of Spain would say to him.

"I have read your request," the king said. "But I am not sure I understand. Do you want to sail to the Spice Islands?"

"Yes, Your Majesty," said Magellan. "If you let me use your ships, I will find a faster and easier way to reach the Spice Islands. I will bring the spices back to Spain."

The king nodded. "I see. But the Spice Islands lie to the east. Why do you plan to sail west?"

"The Earth is round," said Magellan. "If I sail west, sooner or later I will end up in the east."

The king asked many questions. No one had ever sailed around the world. In March 1518, King Charles decided to help Magellan. "I will give you five ships," he said. "But you must find your own crew."

Magellan needed 250 men. Some of his crew were brave and trusted sailors. But Magellan also signed up criminals. They went just to get out of jail.

Magellan set sail in September of 1519. It took his ships two months to cross the Atlantic Ocean. They ran into many storms. At last they reached South America. There they turned south and followed the coast. They were searching for a water passage.

Soon Magellan's men became tired and unhappy. Winter was coming. The men wanted to go home. Magellan would not turn around. "I will die before I will turn back," he said. "We will anchor for the winter. In the spring, we will continue our journey." Some men planned to take over. Magellan put an end to that trouble. But he knew it could happen again.

For five months, Magellan waited for spring. One of his ships was destroyed in a storm. At last he set off again. On October 21, 1520, Magellan saw a wide opening along the coast. He turned his ships into it. It would be later be named the Strait of Magellan.

Go on to the next page.

Circling the World, p. 2

For the next 38 days, Magellan's ships made their way through a tangle of rocks. At times the passage was very narrow. It twisted one way, then another. The men were afraid. On the supply ship, the men gave up. Without telling Magellan, they turned around and sailed home. With them went most of the food.

On November 28, Magellan finally saw open water up ahead. He wept with joy as his ships sailed out into a beautiful blue sea. This ocean seemed so gentle. The men named it the "Pacific." This means *the peaceful sea.*

Magellan thought the Pacific Ocean was about 600 miles wide. He thought he would reach the Spice Islands in a few weeks. In fact, the Pacific Ocean is over 11,000 miles wide. Day after day, he stared into the distance, hoping to see land. But he saw only water.

After two months of this, the group was in terrible shape. The ships creaked and groaned with each wave. New leaks appeared every day. The men had no fresh food. Many of them became sick.

At last, the Spice Islands were only a few hundred miles away.

"I've done it!" Magellan thought happily. "I've found a route all the way around the world."

His men wanted to get home. But they became caught in a war. In a battle on April 27, 1521, Magellan was killed. The men were very sad.

Juan Sebastian del Cano took command. He sailed the three ships on to the Spice Islands. There he decided that only one ship could go on. On September 8, 1522, this ship finally reached Spain. Del Cano fell to his knees in thanks when he saw land. He had lived through the amazing voyage around the world. He was one of only 18 men who had made it.

Go on to the next page.

Circling the World, p. 3

Directions Answer the questions in complete sentences.

1. Name one of the most important ideas from the story.

_____

_____

_____

2. What country did King Charles V rule?

_____

_____

_____

3. How long did it take Magellan to cross the Atlantic Ocean?

_____

_____

_____

4. What is the meaning of *Pacific*?

_____

_____

_____

5. How wide is the Pacific Ocean?

_____

_____

_____

X

Language Arts Overall Assessment

(Directions) For questions 1–3, darken the circle next to the sentence that has the correct capitalization and punctuation.

1. Ⓐ My homeroom teacher is mr. McGraw.
Ⓑ The fireworks at Victoria Park are really special!
Ⓒ Would you like to ski in Vale Colorado?
Ⓓ Yes, Rosie has, a lovely singing voice.

2. Ⓐ "What a beautiful painting!" exclaimed Hugo.
Ⓑ Our plane took off from Kennedy airport
Ⓒ Yes Sara, is my best friend
Ⓓ Will you help me set the table.

3. Ⓐ Mr. chian told us about his trip.
Ⓑ Vincent's cousin, lives in California.
Ⓒ Everyone thought i was Julio's brother.
Ⓓ Uncle Gary goes camping every September.

(Directions) Darken the circle for the underlined word that answers the question. Darken the circle for *D. None of these* if none of the words answers the question.

4. Which of the underlined words is a verb?

It snowed last night. None of these
Ⓐ   Ⓑ   Ⓒ   Ⓓ

5. Which of the underlined words is an adjective?

Garret built a huge sand castle. None of these
Ⓐ   Ⓑ   Ⓒ   Ⓓ

6. Which of the underlined words is a noun?

Mr. Ling says that Amy is a good student. None of these
   Ⓐ   Ⓑ   Ⓒ   Ⓓ

7. Which of the underlined words is a verb?

Rosie always walks home from school. None of these
Ⓐ   Ⓑ   Ⓒ   Ⓓ

Go on to the next page.

X

Language Arts Overall Assessment, p. 2

Directions Write **index**, **glossary**, **table of contents**, or **title page** next to where you think you would look for the following information.

8. the name of the author of a book _____

9. what information is discussed in Chapter 2 _____

10. what the term "cubic" means _____

11. how many pages mention "deserts" _____

Directions Darken the circle for the word that is mispelled. If there are no spelling errors, darken the circle for *D. No mistake*.

12. Birds <u>steak</u> out a <u>territory</u> when they are <u>nesting</u>. No mistake
    Ⓐ   Ⓑ   Ⓒ   Ⓓ

13. Lucia <u>received</u> an <u>imvitation</u> to the <u>birthday</u> party. No mistake
    Ⓐ   Ⓑ   Ⓒ   Ⓓ

Directions For questions 14–16 darken the circle for the simple subject.

14. <u>Janet</u> <u>is</u> my <u>older</u> <u>sister</u>.
    Ⓐ Ⓑ   Ⓒ   Ⓓ

15. <u>We</u> <u>danced</u> and sang at <u>Arthur's</u> <u>party</u>.
    Ⓐ   Ⓑ   Ⓒ   Ⓓ

16. <u>Linda</u> <u>loves</u> to <u>play</u> the <u>piano</u>.
    Ⓐ   Ⓑ   Ⓒ   Ⓓ

Directions For questions 17–20 darken the circle for the simple predicate.

17. There <u>are</u> three <u>children</u> in <u>my</u> <u>family</u>.
    Ⓐ   Ⓑ   Ⓒ Ⓓ

18. <u>Roger</u> <u>is</u> my <u>older</u> <u>brother</u>.
    Ⓐ Ⓑ   Ⓒ   Ⓓ

19. <u>Randy</u> <u>collects</u> rare <u>old</u> <u>coins</u>.
    Ⓐ   Ⓑ   Ⓒ Ⓓ

20. Last <u>week</u> Jorge <u>played</u> in the <u>soccer</u> <u>game</u>.
    Ⓐ   Ⓑ   Ⓒ   Ⓓ

    Assessments to Identify Skills and Needs 4, SV 3395-2

Capitalization

(Directions) Darken the circle for the part of the sentence that needs a capital letter. Darken the circle for *D. None of these* if no capital letter is needed.

1. Robert L. stevenson   is the author of   Treasure Island.   None of these
Ⓐ   Ⓑ   Ⓒ   Ⓓ

2. Roy said,   "let's go outside   to play."   None of these
Ⓐ   Ⓑ   Ⓒ   Ⓓ

3. Juan and i   like to collect   comic books.   None of these
Ⓐ   Ⓑ   Ⓒ   Ⓓ

4. Spring   will begin   on march 21.   None of these
Ⓐ   Ⓑ   Ⓒ   Ⓓ

5. Sunday is   my favorite   day of the week.   None of these
Ⓐ   Ⓑ   Ⓒ   Ⓓ

6. Next year   we will start   to study spanish.   None of these
Ⓐ   Ⓑ   Ⓒ   Ⓓ

7. In london, England,   you can   see Big Ben.   None of these
Ⓐ   Ⓑ   Ⓒ   Ⓓ

8. My favorite   music composer   is brahms.   None of these
Ⓐ   Ⓑ   Ⓒ   Ⓓ

9. Our art teacher   Ms. Morris is   being honored.   None of these
Ⓐ   Ⓑ   Ⓒ   Ⓓ

10. Next year   we'll be going to   middle school.   None of these
Ⓐ   Ⓑ   Ⓒ   Ⓓ

Capitalization

Directions Darken the circle for the part of the passage that has an error in capitalization. Darken the circle for *D. No mistakes* if there are no capitalization errors.

1. Ⓐ I'm sure you'll really like Baxter park.
   Ⓑ Your friend,
   Ⓒ Marissa
   Ⓓ No mistakes

2. Ⓐ Next tuesday afternoon
   Ⓑ we are going shopping
   Ⓒ for party favors.
   Ⓓ No mistakes

3. Ⓐ Will you be going
   Ⓑ to a camp
   Ⓒ this summer?
   Ⓓ No mistakes

4. Ⓐ The Phoenicians
   Ⓑ had to learn a new picture
   Ⓒ for every word they had.
   Ⓓ No mistakes

5. Ⓐ space flights are
   Ⓑ launched from Cape Canaveral
   Ⓒ in the state of Florida.
   Ⓓ No mistakes

6. Ⓐ Dear Kelly,
   Ⓑ I'm so glad that you can
   Ⓒ join us on the hike next week.
   Ⓓ No mistakes

7. Ⓐ 23 Pembrook drive
   Ⓑ North Dartmouth, NY 11590
   Ⓒ June 21, 1999
   Ⓓ No mistakes

8. Ⓐ Our school baseball team
   Ⓑ will play an important game
   Ⓒ on thursday afternoon.
   Ⓓ No mistakes

9. Ⓐ Please come to
   Ⓑ woodland School's fair
   Ⓒ on October 24, 1999.
   Ⓓ No mistakes

10. Ⓐ Lake george
    Ⓑ is one of the most beautiful
    Ⓒ lakes I've ever seen.
    Ⓓ No mistakes

X

Punctuation

Directions Darken the circle for the punctuation mark that makes the sentence correct. Darken the circle for *D. None of these* if no other punctuation is needed.

1. Montreal Canada is the home of the Expos team.

Ⓐ ,

Ⓑ ?

Ⓒ .

Ⓓ None of these

2. We bought notebooks pens, and paper clips at the stationery store.

Ⓐ .

Ⓑ ;

Ⓒ ,

Ⓓ None of these

3. Kevin asked, When do you expect to finish working?"

Ⓐ "

Ⓑ ,

Ⓒ .

Ⓓ None of these

4. Don't slam the door!

Ⓐ :

Ⓑ "

Ⓒ ?

Ⓓ None of these

5. Colin said, This is my favorite toy."

Ⓐ "

Ⓑ !

Ⓒ '

Ⓓ None of these

6. We need pens tagboard, scissors, and glue for our project.

Ⓐ .

Ⓑ ,

Ⓒ !

Ⓓ None of these

7. The American flag is red, white, and blue.

Ⓐ !

Ⓑ "

Ⓒ ;

Ⓓ None of these

8. When are you leaving

Ⓐ ?

Ⓑ .

Ⓒ "

Ⓓ None of these

9. Disney World is in Orlando Florida.

Ⓐ !

Ⓑ ?

Ⓒ ,

Ⓓ None of these

10. Did you enjoy that book

Ⓐ "

Ⓑ !

Ⓒ ?

Ⓓ None of these

Capitalization and Punctuation

Directions Darken the circle for the choice that shows the correct capitalization and punctuation for the underlined part of the passage. Darken the circle for *D. Correct as it is* if there is no error.

1. "Oh," said Beryl, <u>I give up</u>.

  Ⓐ I give up?
  Ⓑ I, give up.
  Ⓒ "I give up."
  Ⓓ Correct as it is

2. Did you watch <u>"The Wizard of Oz"</u> on television?

  Ⓐ "The Wizard of Oz
  Ⓑ The wizard of Oz
  Ⓒ "the Wizard of oz"
  Ⓓ Correct as it is

3. You are invited to attend our <u>annual Holiday concert</u>.

  Ⓐ annual holiday concert.
  Ⓑ Annual Holiday concert.
  Ⓒ annual, holiday concert.
  Ⓓ Correct as it is

4. I want to cut some <u>lilacs, tulips daffodils, and roses</u>.

  Ⓐ lilacs tulips, daffodils, and roses.
  Ⓑ lilacs, tulips, daffodils, and roses.
  Ⓒ lilacs, tulips, daffodils, and, roses.
  Ⓓ Correct as it is

5. Mrs. Robson <u>and mrs. Morales are</u> our class mothers.

  Ⓐ , and Mrs. Morales
  Ⓑ and Mrs. Morales
  Ⓒ and, Mrs. Morales
  Ⓓ Correct as it is

6. Canoe Cove is a village on Prince <u>Edward. Island, Canada</u>.

  Ⓐ Prince Edward Island Canada
  Ⓑ Prince Edward Island, Canada
  Ⓒ Prince Edward Island. Canada
  Ⓓ Correct as it is

7. Mr. Green grows <u>flowers, but</u> he doesn't grow vegetables.

  Ⓐ flowers but, Ⓒ flowers but
  Ⓑ flowers. But Ⓓ Correct as it is

8. Everyone was looking forward to <u>January 1 2001</u>.

  Ⓐ January 1, 2001
  Ⓑ January, 1, 2001
  Ⓒ January, 1 2001
  Ⓓ Correct as it is

9. Toni <u>said I'm going</u> shopping later today."

  Ⓐ said, "I'm going
  Ⓑ said. "I'm going
  Ⓒ said, I'm going
  Ⓓ Correct as it is

10. <u>April 18 2002</u>
Dear Lila
    I'm so sorry that you weren't able to see our school play last week.

  Ⓐ April 18, 2002
  Ⓑ April, 18 2002
  Ⓒ April, 18, 2002
  Ⓓ Correct as it is

Nouns

Directions Underline the two nouns in each sentence.

1. Mrs. Smith has a big job ahead.

2. She needs to plan a picnic for her family.

3. The family always enjoys the picnic.

4. It is a big event every year.

5. Margie will make the hamburgers.

6. Mrs. Smith finally picked Riverview Park.

7. The park is on the Mississippi River.

Directions Tell what each underlined noun is by writing **person**, **place**, or **thing**.

8. _____ the state of <u>Utah</u>

9. _____ my friend's <u>sister</u>

10. _____ 472 <u>Elm Street</u>

11. _____ Morris the <u>cat</u>

12. _____ the city of <u>Trenton</u>

13. _____ <u>Orville's</u> friend

14. _____ presented by the <u>mayor</u>

15. _____ <u>Sydney</u>, Australia

Verbs

(Directions) Darken the circle for the verb that completes the sentence.

1. They ____ each other every summer.

- Ⓐ sees
- Ⓑ visits
- Ⓒ visiting
- Ⓓ visit

2. When will you ____ her again?

- Ⓐ had seen
- Ⓑ seen
- Ⓒ see
- Ⓓ saw

3. I ____ to visit you.

- Ⓐ have came
- Ⓑ came
- Ⓒ had coming
- Ⓓ coming

4. The man said he ____ going to call you later.

- Ⓐ were
- Ⓑ would
- Ⓒ was
- Ⓓ weren't

5. They ____ TV on rainy days.

- Ⓐ watching
- Ⓑ watch
- Ⓒ were watched
- Ⓓ was watching

6. He always ____ his time.

- Ⓐ taken
- Ⓑ taking
- Ⓒ takes
- Ⓓ taked

7. Listen for knocks when the motor is ____.

- Ⓐ run
- Ⓑ ran
- Ⓒ runned
- Ⓓ running

8. My father will ____ home early today.

- Ⓐ be
- Ⓑ been
- Ⓒ had been
- Ⓓ has been

9. Regina and Tony ____ cousins.

- Ⓐ are
- Ⓑ is
- Ⓒ was
- Ⓓ am

10. Todd and I ____ each other.

- Ⓐ seen
- Ⓑ has seen
- Ⓒ saw
- Ⓓ have saw

Pronouns

Directions Darken the circle for the pronoun that completes the sentence.

1. We told ____.

    Ⓐ they   Ⓑ them   Ⓒ he   Ⓓ she

2. ____ heel was broken.

    Ⓐ Her   Ⓑ She   Ⓒ Them   Ⓓ Our

3. That looks like ____ son.

    Ⓐ its   Ⓑ them   Ⓒ their   Ⓓ they

4. The librarian read ____ a very funny book.

    Ⓐ we   Ⓑ ourselves   Ⓒ myself   Ⓓ us

5. Is ____ the one who found the ring?

    Ⓐ she   Ⓑ her   Ⓒ him   Ⓓ his

6. ____ runs in many races.

    Ⓐ We   Ⓑ Him   Ⓒ He   Ⓓ I

7. All of ____ grapes were ripe.

    Ⓐ mine   Ⓑ him   Ⓒ them   Ⓓ my

8. Perry shared his candy with Ethan and ____.

    Ⓐ me   Ⓑ I   Ⓒ she   Ⓓ we

9. Did you ever see the giant tree in ____ backyard?

    Ⓐ their   Ⓑ there   Ⓒ they're   Ⓓ they

10. Rhonda gave ____ a gift.

    Ⓐ him   Ⓑ his   Ⓒ himself   Ⓓ he's

Using Words Correctly

Directions Darken the circle for the word or words that best complete the sentence.

1. The giraffe is the ____ animal.

   Ⓐ tall   Ⓑ taller   Ⓒ tallest   Ⓓ tallness

2. The blue whale is ____ than any other mammal.

   Ⓐ biggest   Ⓑ big   Ⓒ bigly   Ⓓ bigger

3. She plays the piano very ____.

   Ⓐ good   Ⓑ better   Ⓒ well   Ⓓ best

4. Don't you have ____ family?

   Ⓐ any   Ⓑ no   Ⓒ none   Ⓓ no one

5. The phone rang ____.

   Ⓐ sudden   Ⓑ loud   Ⓒ suddenly   Ⓓ jarring

6. Does anyone know if ____ going swimming today?

   Ⓐ where   Ⓑ wear   Ⓒ we're   Ⓓ were

7. This is the ____ sweater I own.

   Ⓐ warmest   Ⓑ warmer   Ⓒ most warm   Ⓓ warm

8. The plane ____ up above the clouds.

   Ⓐ flown   Ⓑ flied   Ⓒ flew   Ⓓ has flew

9. Stacey is ____ how to skate.

   Ⓐ learned   Ⓑ learn   Ⓒ learning   Ⓓ learner

10. That was the ____ birthday cake I ever had!

   Ⓐ bestest   Ⓑ goodest   Ⓒ most best   Ⓓ best

Sentence Parts

Directions Darken the circle for the simple subject.

1. <u>Our</u> <u>teacher</u> is <u>taking</u> us on a <u>field</u> trip.
Ⓐ   Ⓑ   Ⓒ   Ⓓ

2. <u>Are</u> <u>we</u> still <u>going</u> to the <u>magic show</u>?
Ⓐ Ⓑ   Ⓒ   Ⓓ

3. <u>His</u> <u>mother</u> works the <u>night</u> <u>shift</u>.
Ⓐ   Ⓑ   Ⓒ   Ⓓ

4. <u>Every</u> <u>Tuesday</u>, <u>I</u> visit my <u>grandmother</u>.
Ⓐ   Ⓑ   Ⓒ   Ⓓ

5. <u>Do</u> <u>you</u> <u>like</u> to play <u>basketball</u>?
Ⓐ Ⓑ Ⓒ   Ⓓ

Directions Darken the circle for the simple predicate.

6. <u>Our</u> <u>teacher</u> <u>taught</u> us to <u>type</u>.
Ⓐ   Ⓑ   Ⓒ   Ⓓ

7. <u>I</u> <u>went</u> to the <u>Science Club</u> <u>meeting</u>.
Ⓐ Ⓑ   Ⓒ   Ⓓ

8. <u>Close</u> the <u>door</u> <u>quietly</u>, <u>please</u>.
Ⓐ   Ⓑ   Ⓒ   Ⓓ

9. <u>Good</u> <u>students</u> <u>use</u> <u>dictionaries</u>.
Ⓐ   Ⓑ   Ⓒ   Ⓓ

10. <u>Joseph</u> <u>seemed</u> very <u>tired</u> <u>yesterday</u>.
Ⓐ   Ⓑ   Ⓒ   Ⓓ

Clear Sentences

Directions Darken the circle for the sentence that is written most clearly.

1. Ⓐ Our apple tree has apples so many. We'll never eat them all.
   Ⓑ Our apple tree has so many apples that we'll never eat them all.
   Ⓒ All them apples on our tree. We'll never eat them.
   Ⓓ Them apples on our tree. All them we'll never eat.

2. Ⓐ Please phone me as soon as you arrive.
   Ⓑ Please, as soon as you arrive, me phone.
   Ⓒ As soon as you arrive, me please phone.
   Ⓓ Soon please, phone me as you arrive.

3. Ⓐ On the every Wednesday the Student Council will meet.
   Ⓑ The Student Council it will meet every Wednesday.
   Ⓒ Every Wednesday it will meet the Student Council.
   Ⓓ The Student Council will meet every Wednesday.

4. Ⓐ Mrs. Jonas sells pies and cakes in her bakery.
   Ⓑ Pies and cakes is what Mrs. Jonas sells in her bakery.
   Ⓒ In her bakery Mrs. Jonas she sells pies and cake.
   Ⓓ Mrs. Jonas she sells pies and she sells cakes in her bakery.

5. Ⓐ Some children still like to play tag in the schoolyard.
   Ⓑ Some children still like to play in the schoolyard tag.
   Ⓒ In the schoolyard still tag is what some children like to play.
   Ⓓ Tag is what some schoolyard children like still to play.

6. Ⓐ Gregory tried out for the football team last week.
   Ⓑ For the football team he tried out, Gregory.
   Ⓒ Last week Gregory he tried out for the football team.
   Ⓓ Gregory last week tried he out for the football team.

Spelling

Directions Read each sentence. If one of the words is misspelled, darken the circle for that word. If all the words are spelled correctly, then darken the circle for *D. No mistake.*

1. Meryl was <u>dizzy</u> from <u>spinning</u> <u>around</u> so much. <u>No mistake</u>
     Ⓐ   Ⓑ   Ⓒ   Ⓓ

2. Roland <u>enjoys</u> eating <u>cereal</u> with <u>blueberrys</u> in it. <u>No mistake</u>
    Ⓐ   Ⓑ   Ⓒ   Ⓓ

3. Mr. Chung <u>travilled</u> a <u>great</u> deal when he was <u>younger</u>. <u>No mistake</u>
      Ⓐ   Ⓑ   Ⓒ   Ⓓ

4. The <u>fourth</u> grade <u>childrin</u> are going on a <u>field</u> trip next week. <u>No mistake</u>
    Ⓐ   Ⓑ   Ⓒ   Ⓓ

5. <u>Everyone</u> is <u>busy</u> working on a <u>special</u> project. <u>No mistake</u>
  Ⓐ   Ⓑ   Ⓒ   Ⓓ

6. The <u>storm</u> produced <u>driveing</u> rain and <u>hail</u>. <u>No mistake</u>
    Ⓐ   Ⓑ   Ⓒ   Ⓓ

7. Hakim was <u>absint</u> from <u>class</u> on <u>Tuesday</u>. <u>No mistake</u>
      Ⓐ   Ⓑ   Ⓒ   Ⓓ

8. The <u>pair</u> that Beth bought was <u>ripe</u> and <u>sweet</u>. <u>No mistake</u>
    Ⓐ   Ⓑ   Ⓒ   Ⓓ

9. Hugo <u>bought</u> a box of <u>pencils</u> for <u>fourty</u> cents. <u>No mistake</u>
      Ⓐ   Ⓑ   Ⓒ   Ⓓ

10. We <u>allmost</u> lost the <u>directions</u> for making the <u>model</u> plane. <u>No mistake</u>
   Ⓐ   Ⓑ   Ⓒ   Ⓓ

Spelling

Directions Darken the circle for the correctly spelled word that fits the sentence.

1. Our new school ____ will speak to us in the auditorium.
   - (A) prinsipal
   - (B) principle
   - (C) principal
   - (D) principale

2. Zach's ____ will visit him this summer.
   - (A) couzin
   - (B) cousen
   - (C) cusoin
   - (D) cousin

3. Over two ____ people marched in the parade.
   - (A) hundrid
   - (B) hundred
   - (C) hunddred
   - (D) hundered

4. Eating too much ____ is bad for your teeth.
   - (A) suger
   - (B) suggar
   - (C) sugar
   - (D) sugger

5. I hope that we have ____ paint.
   - (A) enough
   - (B) enuogh
   - (C) enouhg
   - (D) enoughe

6. We need a crossing ____ at the intersection.
   - (A) garde
   - (B) guard
   - (C) gaurd
   - (D) grad

7. Do you ____ in monster stories?
   - (A) beleive
   - (B) bellieve
   - (C) believe
   - (D) bilieve

8. Valerie has to ____ the piano.
   - (A) practise
   - (B) pracktice
   - (C) practice
   - (D) praktice

9. Sandy is ____ a letter.
   - (A) writting
   - (B) writing
   - (C) writeing
   - (D) righting

10. My best friend was ____ as class president.
    - (A) elekted
    - (B) elected
    - (C) electid
    - (D) eelected

Spelling

(**Directions**) Learn to spell these words. Use each word in a sentence. Spell these words correctly in all your writing.

about	early	little	raise	tomorrow
address	easy	loose	read	tonight
again	enough	loving	receive	train
all right	every	making	remember	trouble
along	fierce	many	right	truly
already	first	maybe	rough	until
always	forty	mother	said	used
among	fourth	name	says	vacation
because	friend	nice	school	very
been	getting	none	shoes	wear
before	guard	o'clock	since	weather
bought	guess	off	skis	weigh
busy	half	often	some	were
buy	haven't	once	soon	we're
choose	having	party	store	when
close	hear	peace	straight	where
come	heard	people	summer	which
coming	here	piece	sure	white
could	hour	played	teacher	whole
couldn't	house	plays	tear	would
country	instead	please	terrible	write
dear	knew	pretty	they	wrote
desert	know	quarter	thought	your
dessert	laid	quit	through	you're
didn't	letter	quite	tired	

Reference Materials

(Directions) Darken the circle for the correct answer.

1. It is important to write the name of the book and the ____ when writing notes on a note card.

   (A) author   (B) table of contents   (C) glossary   (D) chapter

2. A good writer uses a different ____ for each new question.

   (A) author   (B) encyclopedia   (C) topic   (D) note card

3. You would probably use a(n) ____ to find out about a recent news event.

   (A) encyclopedia   (B) dictionary   (C) computer   (D) book

4. You would probably use a(n) ____ to find out the meaning of a word.

   (A) encyclopedia   (B) dictionary   (C) computer   (D) book

5. To find the meaning of the word *unconscious* in your health book, you would look at the ____.

   (A) glossary   (B) table of contents   (C) index   (D) title page

6. To find the author of the book <u>Exercise to Good Health</u>, you would use the ____ card in a card catalog.

   (A) author   (B) subject   (C) title   (D) glossary

7. A ____ map shows the location of things people use, such as trees or minerals.

   (A) road   (B) resource   (C) precipitation   (D) legend

8. A ____ is a picture that shows the order of historical events.

   (A) table   (B) time line   (C) web   (D) scan

9. You would probably use a(n) ____ to find the map of a country that a famous doctor is from.

   (A) index   (B) atlas   (C) dictionary   (D) thesaurus

10. You would probably use a(n) ____ to find a synonym for the word *sick*.

    (A) index   (B) atlas   (C) dictionary   (D) thesaurus

Parts of a Book

Directions Use the example book pages to answer the questions.

A Number of Stories	**Contents**
by Lisa Newton	Adding It Up 1
	Magic Numbers 10
Brandywine Arts, Inc.	Time Tells All 17
Chicago, Illinois	Triple Trouble...............42
	Millions of Dimes 58

1. What is the title of the book? _____

2. On what page is "Triple Trouble"? _____

3. Who is the publisher of the book? _____

4. Who wrote the book? _____

5. What is the first chapter of the book? _____

---

an·swer {an´sər} *n.* A solution to an arithmetic problem.

a·rith·me·tic {ə·rith´mə·tik} *n.* A kind of mathematics that deals with numbers.

dou·ble {dub´əl} *v.* To make or become twice as much.

glossary

Subtraction
  fractions, 58–60, 119
  whole numbers, 15, 17–20
Word problems
  addition, 2–4, 39
  division, 40–45, 68
  multiplication, 25–33, 62
  subtraction, 19–20, 60

index

---

6. What word means "to make or become twice as much"?

_____

7. On which pages could you find multiplication word problems?

_____

8. On which pages would you find facts about fractions?

_____

9. What is the definition of *answer*?

_____

10. How many pages have information on addition word problems?

_____

Alphabetical Order and Dictionary Skills

Directions Rewrite each group of words in alphabetical order. Then, at the top write the words that would be the guide words for each group.

1. _____ / _____

2. lawn _____

3. last _____

4. lamp _____

5. late _____

6. lap _____

7. lake _____

8. _____ / _____

9. palm _____

10. page _____

11. pass _____

12. pad _____

13. pack _____

14. pan _____

---

club   **detector**

club [klub] *n., v.* **clubbed, clubbing 1** *n.* Heavy wooden stick for use as a weapon, generally thicker at one end. **2** *n.* A stick or bat used to hit a ball: a golf *club*. **3** *n.* A figure like this: ♣ **4** *n.* A playing card of the suit marked with black club figures. **5** *n.* A group of people organized for enjoyment of some purpose: a social *club*.

clue [kloo] *n.* A hint or piece of evidence, helpful in solving a problem or mystery.

D

de·tec·tive [di·tek′tiv] **1** *n.* A person, often a police officer, whose work is to investigate crimes, find out hidden information, and watch suspected persons. **2** *adj.* Of, for, or about detectives and their work: a *detective* story.

---

15. How many entry words are shown in the sample? _____

16. What would the last word on this page be? _____

17. What are the guide words on this page? _____

18. Could the entry word *dog* appear on this page? _____

Charts and Graphs

(Directions) Darken the circle for the correct answer.

Number of Sit-Ups

	Monday	Tuesday	Wednesday	Thursday	Friday
C H I L D R E N Nancy	18	21	23	28	30
Tim	32	40	41	45	47
Larry	21	27	32	34	35
Beth	28	32	35	32	33

1. How many sit-ups did Beth do altogether?
Ⓐ 205   Ⓑ 160   Ⓒ 90   Ⓓ 99

2. How many sit-ups did Beth do on Tuesday?
Ⓐ 28   Ⓑ 35   Ⓒ 21   Ⓓ 32

3. Who did the most sit-ups on Wednesday?
Ⓐ Nancy   Ⓑ Tim   Ⓒ Larry   Ⓓ Beth

4. On what day did Tim do the most sit-ups?
Ⓐ Monday   Ⓑ Thursday   Ⓒ Tuesday   Ⓓ Friday

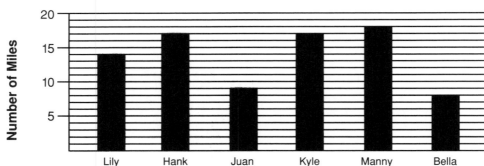

5. How many more miles did Kyle ride than Lily?
Ⓐ 3 miles   Ⓓ 2 miles
Ⓑ 6 miles   Ⓔ None of these
Ⓒ 1 mile

6. What was the total number of miles that the students rode?
Ⓐ 100 miles   Ⓓ 95 miles
Ⓑ 75 miles   Ⓔ None of these
Ⓒ 83 miles

7. How many students rode fewer than 16 miles?
Ⓐ 2 students   Ⓓ 1 student
Ⓑ 3 students   Ⓔ None of these
Ⓒ 4 students

8. Who rode the farthest?
Ⓐ Bella   Ⓓ Manny
Ⓑ Hank   Ⓔ None of these
Ⓒ Juan

Personal Narrative

Directions Read the personal narrative. Then answer the questions.

My great-uncle Daniel had his seventy-fifth birthday last week. He told us an amazing story at his birthday party.

Daniel's Grandpa Weaver had made bricks many years ago. But Daniel and his family were not very interested in bricks. Everyone forgot about Grandpa Weaver's old brick business.

Uncle Daniel and his brothers grew up and moved away. All of them married and had children of their own. Daniel and his wife were schoolteachers for 40 years.

Uncle Daniel and Aunt Ginny built a brick patio in their backyard last summer. Some friends told Uncle Daniel about a place to buy bricks. He and Aunt Ginny drove several miles to look at the bricks. All the bricks lay in a pile near an old house. Uncle Daniel bought several of the bricks. He and Aunt Ginny looked at the bricks in amazement. The name "Weaver" was stamped on them. The bricks had been made by my great-great-grandfather more than 150 years ago!

1. What happens at the end of the narrative?

_____

_____

_____

2. What does the narrative reveal about the writer's great-uncle?

_____

_____

_____

3. What details did the writer use to describe Uncle Daniel and Aunt Ginny?

_____

_____

_____

4. On another sheet of paper, write your own personal narrative.

Information Paragraph

Directions Read the information paragraph. Then answer the questions.

The kangaroos are native to Australia. They carry their young in a pouch. A baby kangaroo is called a joey. Kangaroos are not the only unusual animals that are native to Australia. It is also the home of a huge bird, the emu. The emu is only a little smaller than an ostrich. It eats grass, flowers, insects, and almost anything else. Another strange animal from Australia is the platypus. It looks like a combination of a beaver, a duck, and an otter.

1. What is the topic sentence of the paragraph?

_____

_____

_____

2. List two sentences that give details about the main idea.

_____

_____

_____

_____

_____

3. What does the emu eat?

_____

_____

_____

4. On another sheet of paper, write an information paragraph.

How-To Paragraph

Directions Read the how-to paragraph. Then answer the questions.

"Musical Chairs" is a good game to play with a group of friends. You will need some chairs and a radio or record player. One person should be in charge of starting and stopping the music. First, count the players and subtract one. Then, place that number of chairs in a circle facing outward. Next, the players walk around the circle of chairs as the music plays. When the music stops, each player tries to sit in a chair. The one who is left standing is out of the game. Remove one chair from the circle and continue the game. When only one chair is left, the player who gets it wins the game.

1. What is the topic sentence of the paragraph?

_____

_____

2. What information does the last sentence give?

_____

_____

3. What information does the topic sentence give?

_____

4. What information does the first detail sentence give?

_____

5. What information do the detail sentences in the middle of the paragraph give?

_____

6. On another sheet of paper, write your own how-to paragraph.

Persuasive Paragraph

(**Directions**) Read the persuasive paragraph. Answer the questions that follow.

Every student should be required to read <u>Johnny Tremain</u>. <u>Johnny Tremain</u> is the best book written about early America. Johnny is a young silversmith. The story tells about exciting events of the American Revolution. Students can learn about an important time in American history by reading this book.

1. What point is the writer making in the paragraph?

_____

_____

2. Where does the writer make the point clear?

_____

_____

3. What support does the writer use for her argument?

_____

_____

4. Mark each statement that is a fact with **F** and each statement that is an opinion with **O**.

_____ **a.** The book won the Newbery Award.

_____ **b.** The most fun way to learn history is by reading novels.

_____ **c.** <u>Johnny Tremain</u> is the best book written about early America.

_____ **d.** Johnny is a young silversmith.

_____ **e.** <u>Johnny Tremain</u> was written by Esther Forbes.

5. On another sheet of paper, write your own persuasive paragraph.

Math Overall Assessment

Directions Darken the circle for the correct answer.

1. What is the lowest term for the answer to $\frac{13}{16} - \frac{5}{16}$?

   (A) $\frac{12}{16}$ (C) $\frac{3}{8}$

   (B) $\frac{1}{2}$ (D) $\frac{8}{16}$

2. What is the sum of $0.89 + 2.361$ after each decimal is rounded to the nearest whole number?

   (A) 4
   (B) 1
   (C) 3
   (D) 2

3. Estimate the sum of 19, 21, and 29.

   (A) 50
   (B) 40
   (C) 60
   (D) 70

4. The average person breathes 15 times a minute. How many times does a person breathe in a half hour?

   (A) 30
   (B) 450
   (C) 900
   (D) 45

5. On which shape will the arrow stop the most number of times?

   (A) pentagon
   (B) square
   (C) circle
   (D) triangle

6. Hannah swims 25 laps in an hour. Which number sentence shows how to find how many hours it would take Hannah to swim 100 laps?

   (A) $100 \div 25 = \square$
   (B) $25 \times 100 = \square$
   (C) $\square + 100 = 25$
   (D) $25 - \square = 100$

7. Which is the missing number in this set of equivalent fractions?

   $\frac{3}{4} \times \frac{4}{4} = \frac{\square}{16}$

   (A) 8 (C) 16
   (B) 10 (D) 12

8. Which digital display tells about the time on this clock?

   (A) 4:29
   (B) 6:20
   (C) 4:22
   (D) 6:35

9. Charlie has $3.00 to spend at the movies. If he buys a drink for $0.78 and popcorn for $1.27, how much money will he have left?

   (A) $2.05 (C) $1.05
   (B) $0.95 (D) $0.85

10. Which of these numbers is greater than the others?

   (A) 867 (C) 876
   (B) 853 (D) 870

Go on to the next page.

Math Overall Assessment, p. 2

Directions
Darken the circle for the correct answer.

11. What shape comes next in the series?

 Ⓐ   Ⓑ   Ⓒ

12. 78,321
  +   89

Ⓐ 79,400
Ⓑ 78,400
Ⓒ 78,410
Ⓓ 79,369

13. Round 526 to the nearest ten.

Ⓐ 500
Ⓑ 530
Ⓒ 520
Ⓓ 600

14. Estimate the time it takes to set up a tent.

Ⓐ 15 minutes
Ⓑ 5 hours
Ⓒ 5 days
Ⓓ 10 seconds

15. Earl took a bike trip. He rode 46 miles one day and 49 miles the next day. How many miles did he ride altogether?

Ⓐ 83
Ⓑ 95
Ⓒ 109
Ⓓ 85

16. $16.40
  −   3.98

Ⓐ $12.42
Ⓑ $12.52
Ⓒ $13.42
Ⓓ $20.38

Directions
Write the answers.

17.

What is the time when it is 30 minutes before 8:15 A.M.?

_____

18. Complete the pattern.

3, 3, 6, 9, 15, _____, _____,

_____, _____.

Number Concepts

Directions Darken the circle by the correct answer to each problem.

1. Which of these is another way to write 20,483?

  Ⓐ 20,000 + 400 + 80 + 3
  Ⓑ 20,000 + 438 + 3
  Ⓒ 20,000 + 48 + 83
  Ⓓ 20,000 + 84 + 3

2. Which of these number sentences is true?

  Ⓐ 4,156 > 4,257
  Ⓑ 8,651 = 8,000 + 600 + 15
  Ⓒ 375 < 379
  Ⓓ 1,332 > 1,432

3. Which number is two thousand six hundred sixty-four?

  Ⓐ 2,646
  Ⓑ 2,604
  Ⓒ 2,664
  Ⓓ 26,604

4. Which of these groups of numbers is ordered from greatest to smallest?

  Ⓐ 652, 745, 29
  Ⓑ 29, 652, 745
  Ⓒ 745, 652, 29
  Ⓓ 745, 29, 645

5. What is another way to write the numeral in the box?

One thousand seventeen

  Ⓐ 117
  Ⓑ 1,107
  Ⓒ 1,117
  Ⓓ 1,017

6. What does the 4 in 9,742 mean?

  Ⓐ four hundred
  Ⓑ four
  Ⓒ forty
  Ⓓ four thousand

7. Which number sentence belongs to the same fact family as $8 \times 4 = \square$?

  Ⓐ $8 \div \square = 4$
  Ⓑ $8 \div 4 = \square$
  Ⓒ $\square \div 4 = 8$
  Ⓓ $4 \div \square = 8$

8. Estimate the sum of 619 + 296.

  Ⓐ 900
  Ⓑ 800
  Ⓒ 920
  Ⓓ 890

9. What number should come next?

  15, 18, 24, 36, ____

  Ⓐ 37
  Ⓑ 40
  Ⓒ 48
  Ⓓ 60

10. Which of these is the same as DCXXVI?

  Ⓐ 525
  Ⓑ 621
  Ⓒ 1,521
  Ⓓ 626

Number Concepts

Directions Darken the circle by the correct answer to each problem.

1. What is the missing number in this pattern?

50, 45, 40, ____, 30, 25

- Ⓐ 41
- Ⓑ 39
- Ⓒ 35
- Ⓓ 31

2. Which numeral makes this sentence true?

$249 < \square$

- Ⓐ 214
- Ⓒ 241
- Ⓑ 237
- Ⓓ 256

3. What number makes this number sentence true?

$(4 + 6) + 2 = (6 + \square) + 2$

- Ⓐ 0
- Ⓑ 2
- Ⓒ 4
- Ⓓ 6

4. What decimal shows the part of this figure that is shaded?

- Ⓐ 0.058
- Ⓑ 0.58
- Ⓒ 0.42
- Ⓓ 5.8

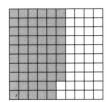

5. Which of the following numbers is odd?

- Ⓐ 138
- Ⓒ 756
- Ⓑ 413
- Ⓓ 294

6. Which figure is missing in this pattern?

☆ ☆ ○ ○ △ _ □ □

- Ⓐ star
- Ⓑ square
- Ⓒ circle
- Ⓓ triangle

7. Which number goes in the box on the number line?

- Ⓐ 180
- Ⓑ 200
- Ⓒ 210
- Ⓓ 190

150   170   □   230 240

8. Which of the following numbers is even?

- Ⓐ 336
- Ⓒ 729
- Ⓑ 873
- Ⓓ 645

9. What number makes both number sentences true?

$0 \div 5 = ?$

$? \times 7 = 0$

- Ⓐ 0
- Ⓑ 5
- Ⓒ 7
- Ⓓ 35

10. Which of these numbers is greater than the others?

- Ⓐ 552
- Ⓑ 549
- Ⓒ 556
- Ⓓ 555

Addition and Subtraction of Whole Numbers

(**Directions**) Darken the circle for the correct answer. Darken the circle for
D. None of these if the answer is _not_ given.

1.   495
    830
  + 185
   ————

  Ⓐ 1,610
  Ⓑ 1,500
  Ⓒ 1,600
  Ⓓ None of these

2. 165 + 202 =

  Ⓐ 376
  Ⓑ 367
  Ⓒ 327
  Ⓓ None of these

3. 1,043 + 6,807 =

  Ⓐ 7,859
  Ⓑ 7,850
  Ⓒ 7,749
  Ⓓ None of these

4.   535
  + 344
   ————

  Ⓐ 879
  Ⓑ 271
  Ⓒ 889
  Ⓓ None of these

5. 307 + 28 + 459 =

  Ⓐ 894
  Ⓑ 1,046
  Ⓒ 794
  Ⓓ 774

6. 1,969
  − 855
  ————

  Ⓐ 914
  Ⓑ 1,114
  Ⓒ 1,104
  Ⓓ None of these

7. 10,360
  −   2
  ————

  Ⓐ 10,362
  Ⓑ 10,358
  Ⓒ 10,368
  Ⓓ None of these

8.   34,898
  − 1,289
  ————

  Ⓐ 33,609
  Ⓑ 34, 610
  Ⓒ 33,619
  Ⓓ None of these

9. 5,078 − 609 =

  Ⓐ 4,469
  Ⓑ 4,568
  Ⓒ 4,669
  Ⓓ None of these

10. 152 − 143 =

  Ⓐ 295
  Ⓑ 19
  Ⓒ 298
  Ⓓ None of these

Name _____ Date _____

Multiplication and Division of Whole Numbers

Directions) Darken the circle for the correct answer. Darken the circle for
D. *None of these* if the correct answer is *not* given.

1. $53 \times 70 =$

Ⓐ 3,710
Ⓑ 37,210
Ⓒ 7,210
Ⓓ None of these

2. $8 \times 7 =$

Ⓐ 15
Ⓑ 51
Ⓒ 56
Ⓓ None of these

3.   11
   $\times\,97$

Ⓐ 1,000
Ⓑ 1,067
Ⓒ 1,097
Ⓓ 197

4. $79 \times 24 =$

Ⓐ 1,896
Ⓑ 1,836
Ⓒ 134
Ⓓ None of these

5.   572
   $\times\,468$

Ⓐ 267,686
Ⓑ 67,696
Ⓒ 167,696
Ⓓ 267,696

6. $60 \div 2 =$

Ⓐ 120
Ⓑ 180
Ⓒ 30
Ⓓ None of these

7. $7\overline{)77}$

Ⓐ 10
Ⓑ 7
Ⓒ 11
Ⓓ None of these

8. $568 \div 9 =$

Ⓐ 64
Ⓑ 63 R3
Ⓒ 63 R2
Ⓓ 63 R1

9. $15\overline{)3,115}$

Ⓐ 208
Ⓑ 207 R10
Ⓒ 209
Ⓓ 315

10. $63 \div 9 =$

Ⓐ 9
Ⓑ 7
Ⓒ 8
Ⓓ None of these

Mixed Operations with Whole Numbers

Directions Darken the circle for the correct answer. Darken the circle for
D. None of these if the correct answer is *not* given.

1. $1,489
  − 649

 Ⓐ $1,840
 Ⓑ $1,440
 Ⓒ $850
 Ⓓ None of these

2. □ + 46 = 73

 Ⓐ 119
 Ⓑ 39
 Ⓒ 27
 Ⓓ None of these

3. 6)2,420

 Ⓐ 403 R2
 Ⓑ 413 R1
 Ⓒ 432
 Ⓓ None of these

4. 7 × □ = 42

 Ⓐ 49
 Ⓑ 9
 Ⓒ 6
 Ⓓ None of these

5. 42 + □ = 79

 Ⓐ 37
 Ⓑ 39
 Ⓒ 121
 Ⓓ None of these

6. 4)534

 Ⓐ 113 R1
 Ⓑ 131
 Ⓒ 133 R2
 Ⓓ None of these

7. 46 − 28 =

 Ⓐ 14
 Ⓑ 18
 Ⓒ 24
 Ⓓ None of these

8. 23
  × 15

 Ⓐ 138
 Ⓑ 327
 Ⓒ 345
 Ⓓ None of these

9. $1,693
  − 582

 Ⓐ $873
 Ⓑ $1,111
 Ⓒ $2,275
 Ⓓ None of these

10. 807
  × 60

 Ⓐ 8,670
 Ⓑ 48,240
 Ⓒ 48,640
 Ⓓ None of these

Name _____ Date _____

Geometry

Directions Darken the circle for the correct answer to each question.

1. Which two figures below are congruent?

Ⓐ 1 and 2   Ⓒ 2 and 4
Ⓑ 2 and 3   Ⓓ 1 and 3

2. How many angles does this figure have?

Ⓐ 5 angles
Ⓑ 8 angles
Ⓒ 4 angles
Ⓓ 6 angles

3. What is the name of the figure shown here?

Ⓐ octagon
Ⓑ quadrilateral
Ⓒ hexagon
Ⓓ pentagon

4. How many vertices (the plural of vertex) does a rectangle have?

Ⓐ 3   Ⓒ 4
Ⓑ 5   Ⓓ 2

5. Which picture shows parallel lines?

6. Which of these shows a line of symmetry?

Ⓐ   Ⓑ   Ⓒ   Ⓓ

7. Which of these line segments intersect?

Ⓐ AB and EF   Ⓒ CD and GH
Ⓑ AB and GH   Ⓓ EF and GH

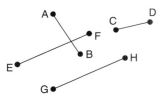

8. What kind of angle is this?

Ⓐ obtuse angle
Ⓑ acute angle
Ⓒ right angle
Ⓓ left angle

9. Which of these figures has a right angle?

Ⓐ   Ⓒ
Ⓑ   Ⓓ

10. What is the letter name of the radius in this circle?

Ⓐ XZ
Ⓑ XYZ
Ⓒ ZX
Ⓓ YZ

Measurement

Directions Darken the circle for the correct answer to each problem.

1. Which unit of measure would you use to describe the weight of a watermelon?

    (A) gram
    (B) liter
    (C) kilogram
    (D) centimeter

2. Which unit of measure describes the length of a letter?

    (A) feet
    (B) inches
    (C) yards
    (D) miles

3. What is the temperature on this thermometer?

    (A) 68°
    (B) 72°
    (C) 70°
    (D) 69°

    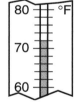

4. How many inches long is rod C?

    (A) $4\frac{1}{2}$ inches
    (B) 2 inches
    (C) $1\frac{1}{2}$ inches
    (D) $3\frac{1}{2}$ inches

    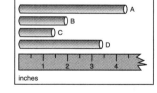

5. Which unit of measurement is best to use to find out how much a tractor weighs?

    (A) ounces
    (B) rods
    (C) inches
    (D) pounds

6. Which of these has a length that is best measured in feet?

    (A) a book   (C) a hamster
    (B) a nail   (D) a bicycle

7. What would be the best unit to use to measure the amount of juice in a pitcher?

    (A) meter   (C) kilometer
    (B) liter   (D) gram

8. How many centimeters are there between point J and point K?

    (A) $1\frac{1}{2}$
    (B) 3
    (C) $3\frac{1}{2}$
    (D) 5

    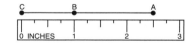

9. How many inches are there between point B and point A?

    (A) $1\frac{1}{2}$ inches
    (B) 3 inches
    (C) 1 inch
    (D) $2\frac{1}{2}$ inches

10. Which would be the best unit to measure the amount of water in a bathtub?

    (A) cups
    (B) gallons
    (C) quarts
    (D) ounces

Name _____ Date _____

Fractions and Decimals

Directions Darken the circle by the correct answer to each problem.

1. $\frac{1}{8}$ of 320 =

   Ⓐ 4   Ⓒ 44

   Ⓑ 40   Ⓓ 80

2. Which shaded part represents the smallest fraction?

   Ⓐ 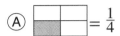 $= \frac{1}{4}$ Ⓒ 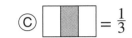 $= \frac{1}{3}$

   Ⓑ 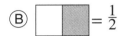 $= \frac{1}{2}$ Ⓓ 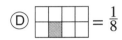 $= \frac{1}{8}$

3. What fraction of this triangle is shaded?

   Ⓐ $\frac{1}{3}$

   Ⓑ $\frac{1}{4}$

   Ⓒ $\frac{2}{3}$

   Ⓓ $\frac{1}{2}$

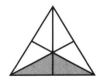

4. Change $2\frac{2}{3}$ into an improper fraction.

   Ⓐ $\frac{8}{3}$

   Ⓑ $\frac{7}{3}$

   Ⓒ $\frac{5}{2}$

   Ⓓ $\frac{22}{3}$

5. $7\frac{3}{20} + 5\frac{7}{20} =$

   Ⓐ $12\frac{2}{20}$

   Ⓑ $12\frac{1}{2}$

   Ⓒ $12\frac{4}{5}$

   Ⓓ $12\frac{4}{20}$

6. Which decimal number has a 4 in the tens place, a three in the ones place, and a five in the hundredths place?

   Ⓐ 43.05

   Ⓑ 534.00

   Ⓒ 53.40

   Ⓓ 4.305

7. Which number sentence is true?

   Ⓐ 0.8 < 0.80

   Ⓑ 0.8 = 0.80

   Ⓒ 0.8 > 0.80

   Ⓓ 0.8 = 0.08

8.   4.68
      + 2.85
      —————

   Ⓐ 7.53

   Ⓑ 70.53

   Ⓒ 753

   Ⓓ 75.30

9. Which decimal shows how much of this group is shaded?

   Ⓐ 1.9

   Ⓑ 0.01

   Ⓒ 1.01

   Ⓓ 1.1

10. 4.622 × 100 =

   Ⓐ 462.2

   Ⓑ 46.22

   Ⓒ 46.022

   Ⓓ 4.622

Statistics and Probability

Directions Write the answers to the questions. Use the table.

Favorite Pets in Mrs. Kohl's Class

Pet	Tally
Cat	ⅢⅢ ⅢⅢ ⅡⅠ
Dog	ⅢⅢ ⅢⅢ ⅢⅠ
Bird	ⅢⅢ
Turtle	ⅢⅠ
Horse	ⅢⅠ

1. Which pet is most popular?

_____

2. How many students like dogs and horses?

_____

3. How many students participated in the survey?

_____

4. What is the probability that a student likes cats?

_____

Directions Darken the circle for the correct answer.

5. Calvin is playing a game using the spinner shown here. If it is spun 7 times, which month will it probably point to least often?

   Ⓐ April
   Ⓑ May
   Ⓒ June
   Ⓓ December

6. If the spinner shown here is spun 8 times, which number will it probably point to most often?

   Ⓐ 4
   Ⓑ 3
   Ⓒ 2
   Ⓓ 1

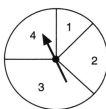

7. Brendan is playing a game. If he spins the arrow 5 times, which letter will it probably stop on most often?

   Ⓐ A
   Ⓑ B
   Ⓒ C
   Ⓓ D

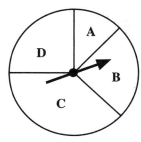

Pre-Algebra: Patterns

Directions Complete each sequence.

1. 1, 1, 2, 3, 5, _____, _____, _____, _____

2. 2, 2, 4, 6, 10, _____, _____, _____, _____

Directions Write the next three numbers in each series by doubling.

3. 3, 6, 12, 24, _____, _____, _____

4. 5, 10, 20, 40, _____, _____, _____

Directions Darken the circle by the correct answer to the problem.

5. What number should come next?

 2, 4, 8, 16, ____

 Ⓐ 18
 Ⓑ 24
 Ⓒ 32
 Ⓓ 40

6. If you continue this pattern, how many dots would the next group have?

 Ⓐ 5 more dots
 Ⓑ 4 more dots
 Ⓒ 3 more dots
 Ⓓ 6 more dots

7. Which number completes the pattern? 5,002; ____; 4,978; 4,966

 Ⓐ 5,014
 Ⓑ 4,990
 Ⓒ 4,986
 Ⓓ 4,954

8. Which number represents the amount of blocks that should be used next in this pattern?

 Ⓐ 14
 Ⓑ 16
 Ⓒ 22
 Ⓓ 17

9. Which group of numbers is made up of multiples of 3?

 Ⓐ 2, 4, 6
 Ⓑ 25, 30, 35
 Ⓒ 18, 21, 24
 Ⓓ 14, 16, 20

10. What number completes this number pattern?

 7, 14, 21, 28, ____

 Ⓐ 42
 Ⓑ 35
 Ⓒ 32
 Ⓓ 30

Pre-Algebra: Patterns

(Directions) Darken the letter for the next shape in the sequence.

1.  Ⓐ ◯ Ⓑ ▢ Ⓒ ◯

(Directions) Draw the next shape in the sequence.

2.  _____

3.  _____

4. _____

5. _____

6. _____

Money

Directions Compare each pocket of change. Write >, <, or = between each set of pockets.

1.
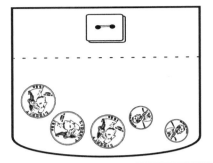

_____

2.
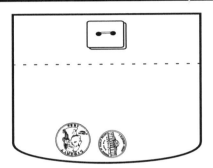

_____

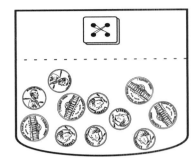

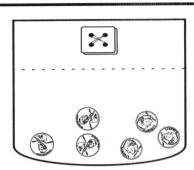

Directions Solve.

3. You paid  . The item cost  .

change: _____

Directions Darken the circle for the correct answer.

4. $0.45
    + 0.83

Ⓐ $1.28
Ⓑ $2.28
Ⓒ 0.78
Ⓓ $1.82

5. 23)$7.82

Ⓐ 34
Ⓑ $34
Ⓒ $3.40
Ⓓ $0.34

6. $1.25
    × 30

Ⓐ $37.50
Ⓑ $375.00
Ⓒ $37.05
Ⓓ $31.25

7. $5.00
    − 4.77

Ⓐ $3.20
Ⓑ $2.30
Ⓒ $0.23
Ⓓ $1.23

Name _____ Date _____

Time

Directions Use the calendar to answer exercises 1 and 2.

❀ ❀ ❀ *May* ❀ ❀ ❀						
Sun	Mon	Tues	Wed	Thurs	Fri	Sat
		1	2	3	4	5
6	7	8	9	10	11	12
13	14	15	16	17	18	19
20	21	22	23	24	25	26
27	28	29	30	31		

1. Write the date of the first Sunday. _____

2. Write the date of the second Monday. _____

Directions Tell how much time has elapsed.

3.

Begin A.M.   End P.M.

_____

Directions Choose the most reasonable unit of time for each: write **seconds**, **minutes**, **hours**, **days**, **weeks**, **months**, or **years**.

4. Summer lasts about 3 _____.

5. It takes about 10 _____ to take a shower.

6. To eat your breakfast takes about 20 _____.

Directions Use the clocks to answer the questions.

7.

How many hours pass from
9:00 A.M. to 2:00 P.M.?

_____

8.

How many minutes pass from
1:20 A.M. to 1:55 P.M.?

_____

Math: Time
Assessments to Identify Skills and Needs 4, SV 3395-2

Name _____ Date _____

Estimation

Directions What would the temperature be outside if you were wearing these clothes? Circle the better estimate for each picture.

1. a.    78°F

50°F

b.    45°C

3°C

Directions How long would each take? Circle the better estimate for each.

2. a.

feeding a cat

3 minutes   15 minutes

b.

walking to school

2 hours   15 minutes

c.

putting a letter in the mailbox

2 seconds   5 minutes

Directions Darken the circle for the correct answer to each question.

3. Which numbers should you use to estimate 494 + 176?

Ⓐ 400 + 200
Ⓑ 500 + 200
Ⓒ 500 + 100
Ⓓ 400 + 100

4. Round 526 to the nearest ten.

Ⓐ 500   Ⓒ 520
Ⓑ 530   Ⓓ 600

5. Estimate the difference between 81 and 49.

Ⓐ 30   Ⓒ 50
Ⓑ 40   Ⓓ 60

6. Estimate the product of 38 × 4.

Ⓐ 120   Ⓒ 160
Ⓑ 110   Ⓓ 180

7. Round 428 to the nearest hundred.

Ⓐ 400   Ⓒ 300
Ⓑ 500   Ⓓ 450

8. Eliot enjoys exercise. It usually takes him 9 minutes to jog a mile. Which is the closest estimate of how long it would take Eliot to jog 5 miles?

Ⓐ Between 20 and 30 minutes
Ⓑ Between 30 and 40 minutes
Ⓒ Between 40 and 50 minutes
Ⓓ Between 50 and 60 minutes

Problem Solving: Whole Numbers

(Directions) Darken the circle for the correct answer to the problem.

1. A bookrack has 4 shelves and contains 168 books. If the books are evenly divided on the shelves, how many books are on each shelf?

   Ⓐ 38   Ⓒ 164
   Ⓑ 42   Ⓓ 151

2. Lorna has 21 yards of fabric to make a bedspread and curtains. If she uses 4 yards to make curtains and 13 yards for the bedspread, how many yards of fabric will she have left?

   Ⓐ 17 yards   Ⓒ 8 yards
   Ⓑ 4 yards   Ⓓ 9 yards

3. Eliza has 47 CDs of pop music and 36 CDs of country music. How many CDs does she have altogether?

   Ⓐ 11   Ⓒ 83
   Ⓑ 53   Ⓓ 60

4. Sandy has $30.00. She wants to buy 2 CDs at the music store. The CDs cost $15.53 each. How much more money does she need to buy both CDs?

   Ⓐ $2.00   Ⓒ $11.06
   Ⓑ $1.06   Ⓓ $0.60

5. A group of 18 friends wants to go camping. If each tent holds 3 people, how many tents will they need?

   Ⓐ 6   Ⓒ 10
   Ⓑ 8   Ⓓ 7

6. Ryan scored 129 points in his first game at the bowling alley and 132 points in his second game. How many points did Ryan score altogether?

   Ⓐ 251   Ⓒ 369
   Ⓑ 261   Ⓓ 161

7. Kyra's dog weighs 38 pounds. Her brother's dog weighs 23 pounds. How much heavier is Kyra's dog than her brother's dog?

   Ⓐ 5 pounds   Ⓒ 24 pounds
   Ⓑ 17 pounds   Ⓓ 15 pounds

8. Mrs. Robinson's class is planning a science fair. They will have 24 exhibits on 4 tables. How many exhibits will they have on each table?

   Ⓐ 20 exhibits Ⓒ 28 exhibits
   Ⓑ 6 exhibits   Ⓓ 16 exhibits

9. There are 30 days in September, November, and June, and 31 days in March. How many days are there in all 4 months?

   Ⓐ 100 days   Ⓒ 121 days
   Ⓑ 120 days   Ⓓ 110 days

10. Ian is 61 inches tall. Tomaso is 52 inches tall. How many inches taller is Ian than Tomaso?

    Ⓐ 10 inches   Ⓒ 9 inches
    Ⓑ 2 inches   Ⓓ 12 inches

Problem Solving: Whole Numbers

Directions Darken the circle for the correct answer to the problem.

1. Joey rides his bicycle 45 minutes every day. How many minutes will he ride in 7 days?

Ⓐ 52 minutes Ⓒ 457 minutes
Ⓑ 315 minutes Ⓓ None of these

2. At Winthrop Middle School, 748 students will be taking achievement tests in the gymnasium. If the custodians place 34 rows of chairs in the gymnasium, how many students will sit in each row?

Ⓐ 25 students Ⓒ 30 students
Ⓑ 22 students Ⓓ 18 students

3. Dominic bought a soccer ball for $9.45 and a basketball for $7.99. Without including tax, how much did he spend altogether?

Ⓐ $13.69 Ⓒ $17.44
Ⓑ $16.55 Ⓓ None of these

4. Kevin delivers pizzas for Rose's Pizza House. On Sunday he delivered 9 pizzas. On Monday he delivered 6 pizzas, and on Tuesday he delivered 12 pizzas. How many pizzas did he deliver in the three days?

Ⓐ 15 pizzas Ⓒ 27 pizzas
Ⓑ 18 pizzas Ⓓ 21 pizzas

5. Dennis bought 4 tapes that cost $2.85, $3.74, $2.94, and $4.35. What was the average cost of each tape?

Ⓐ $3.47 Ⓒ $3.15
Ⓑ $4.23 Ⓓ $2.98

6. Noriko is 53 inches tall, and her younger brother Yuji is 39 inches tall. How much taller is Noriko?

Ⓐ 14 inches Ⓒ 32 inches
Ⓑ 26 inches Ⓓ 24 inches

7. Stella's dog had 4 litters of puppies. Of these puppies, one litter had 5 puppies and three litters had 6 puppies each. How many puppies did Stella's dog have altogether?

Ⓐ 23 puppies Ⓒ 13 puppies
Ⓑ 18 puppies Ⓓ 10 puppies

8. Mr. Collins sold 108 passes last week and 134 passes this week for the riverboat rides. Each pass cost $5.00. How much money did he collect altogether?

Ⓐ $1,210 Ⓒ $670
Ⓑ $1,100 Ⓓ $540

9. Ling read 110 pages of a novel on Friday and 216 pages on Saturday. If it takes her about 3 minutes to read a page of that book, how many minutes did she spend reading on Friday and Saturday altogether?

Ⓐ 326 Ⓒ 672
Ⓑ 330 Ⓓ 978

10. Meg's sticker album has 36 pages. She would like to put 12 stickers on each page. How many stickers will she need to fill the album?

Ⓐ 38 Ⓒ 378
Ⓑ 432 Ⓓ 492

Problem Solving: Measurement and Geometry

Directions Darken the circle for the correct answer to the problem.

1. Which of these has $\frac{1}{4}$ of its area shaded?

Ⓐ A
Ⓑ B
Ⓒ C
Ⓓ D

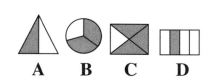

A   B   C   D

2. Iris drew a picture of a swimming pool. What is its perimeter in feet?

Ⓐ 24
Ⓑ 28
Ⓒ 22
Ⓓ 20

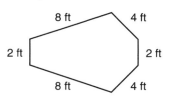

8 ft   4 ft
2 ft   2 ft
8 ft   4 ft

3. Which of these shapes is a hexagon?

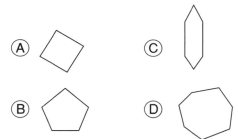

Ⓐ
Ⓒ
Ⓑ
Ⓓ

4. Which statement about this drawing is true?

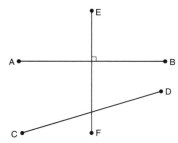

Ⓐ AB is parallel to CD.
Ⓑ AB is perpendicular to EF.
Ⓒ CD is perpendicular to EF.
Ⓓ EF is parallel to AB.

5. Ian measured 2.568 inches of rain in September, 2.674 inches of rain in October, 2.439 inches of rain in November, and 2.136 inches of rain in December. During which month did it rain most?

Ⓐ September
Ⓑ October
Ⓒ November
Ⓓ December

6. Raoul has saved $3.10 to buy a new baseball glove. He needs five times that amount for the glove. How much does the glove cost?

Ⓐ $5.10
Ⓑ $51.00
Ⓒ $15.00
Ⓓ $15.50

7. What time is it 3 hours after 11:00 A.M.?

Ⓐ 2 P.M.
Ⓑ 2 A.M.
Ⓒ 1 P.M.
Ⓓ 1 A.M.

8. Mrs. Garza offered to make lemonade for the school picnic. She plans to make 20 quarts. How many gallons of lemonade will Mrs. Garza make?

Ⓐ 10 gallons
Ⓑ 5 gallons
Ⓒ 3 gallons
Ⓓ 8 gallons

Problem Solving: Fractions and Decimals

Directions Solve each problem. Write the answer.

1. Ilya wants to buy a radio. Each week she saves $\frac{65}{100}$ of her $1.00 allowance. How much does Illya save each week?

_____

2. Once Ilya buys the radio, she tunes into her favorite radio stations. One is located at 94.7 and the other is at 97.3. Which station is closer to 102.3?

_____

3. The radio Ilya wants to buy costs $11.99. She helps her neighbor rake leaves and earns $8.25. How much more money does Ilya need to buy the radio?

_____

4. In a carton of zinnias, $\frac{3}{4}$ of them are red. The rest are white. What fraction are white?

_____

5. The animal shelter has 3 white kittens, 2 gray kittens, and 5 striped kittens. What fraction of kittens at the animal shelter are gray?

_____

6. Janna has $4\frac{2}{3}$ yards of blue fabric. She uses $1\frac{1}{3}$ yards to make a flag. How much fabric does Janna have left?

_____

7. A package of turkey slices sells for $4.68 each or 2 packages for $9.04. Which is the better buy?

_____

8. Find the difference between $4\frac{7}{12}$ and $3\frac{1}{2}$.

_____

Name _____ Date _____

Science Overall Assessment

Directions Darken the circle for the correct answer.

1. How does a prism separate colors?

  Ⓐ It bends each color a different amount.

  Ⓑ It bends each color the same amount.

  Ⓒ It bends only violet.

  Ⓓ It bends only violet and red.

2. Sound waves ____.

  Ⓐ move through matter

  Ⓑ spread out in all directions

  Ⓒ start when a vibration is produced

  Ⓓ all of the above

3. Which of the following is a wheel and axle?

  Ⓐ hammer

  Ⓑ screwdriver

  Ⓒ scissors

  Ⓓ nail

4. We can see the Moon because ____.

  Ⓐ it reflects light it gets from the stars

  Ⓑ it makes its own light

  Ⓒ it reflects light it gets from the Sun

  Ⓓ the Earth reflects light from the Sun

5. Fish are fitted to live in the ocean because they have ____.

  Ⓐ eyes   Ⓒ gills

  Ⓑ bones   Ⓓ nose

6. The water cycle is ____.

  Ⓐ the movement of water between the air and the ground

  Ⓑ a form of transportation

  Ⓒ a weather symbol

  Ⓓ an air mass

7. Erosion occurs when ____.

  Ⓐ soil is added to the ground

  Ⓑ dams are built

  Ⓒ rocks and soil are carried away by wind and water

  Ⓓ grass and trees are planted

8. What changes in a rock during physical weathering?

  Ⓐ color

  Ⓑ size and shape

  Ⓒ the inside of the rock

  Ⓓ nothing

9. Sound is made when an object ____.

  Ⓐ is held

  Ⓑ vibrates

  Ⓒ cools

  Ⓓ stops

10. Within populations, ____ can vary a great deal.

  Ⓐ instincts

  Ⓑ traits

  Ⓒ location

  Ⓓ all of the above

Earth and Space Science

Directions Darken the circle for the correct answer.

1. Humidity is the amount of ____.

   Ⓐ oxygen in the air
   Ⓑ water vapor in the air
   Ⓒ dust in the air
   Ⓓ rain that falls

2. The two main gases in the Earth's atmosphere are nitrogen and ____.

   Ⓐ oxygen
   Ⓑ water vapor
   Ⓒ carbon dioxide
   Ⓓ hydrogen

3. Material carried by rivers to the ocean is called ____.

   Ⓐ rust
   Ⓑ deltas
   Ⓒ sediment
   Ⓓ carbon dioxide

4. A group of billions of stars is called a ____.

   Ⓐ galaxy
   Ⓑ solar system
   Ⓒ constellation
   Ⓓ meteor shower

5. A storm with heavy rains and electric charges jumping from the clouds is a ____.

   Ⓐ blizzard
   Ⓑ hurricane
   Ⓒ thunderstorm
   Ⓓ tornado

6. For a solar eclipse to occur, what has to happen?

   Ⓐ The Moon has to pass between the Earth and the Sun.
   Ⓑ The Earth has to pass between the Moon and the Sun.
   Ⓒ The Sun has to pass between the Earth and the Moon.
   Ⓓ The Moon has to be full.

7. Water vapor changes into a liquid when the air gets ____.

   Ⓐ wetter   Ⓒ warmer
   Ⓑ cooler   Ⓓ drier

8. Clouds, rain, air temperature, and wind are all part of the Earth's ____.

   Ⓐ core
   Ⓑ plates
   Ⓒ ionosphere
   Ⓓ weather

9. The layer of the Earth that is the hottest is the ____.

   Ⓐ core
   Ⓑ mantle
   Ⓒ crust
   Ⓓ surface

10. A machine that measures earthquakes is a ____.

    Ⓐ seismograph
    Ⓑ telegraph
    Ⓒ telescope
    Ⓓ phonograph

Earth and Space Science, p. 2

Directions Answer each question with a complete sentence.

1. Identify something that is a solid, something that is a liquid, and something that is a gas.

_____

_____

_____

2. What are some differences between hurricanes and tornadoes?

_____

_____

_____

3. Which gas makes up the largest part of air?

_____

_____

4. Why do you think people keep track of weather data?

_____

_____

_____

_____

5. What causes a solar eclipse?

_____

_____

_____

Life Science

Directions Write the letter of each word next to its clue.

_____ **1.** how plants make their own food

_____ **2.** grows on food when its spoils

_____ **3.** they move by floating, flying, or sticking to animals

_____ **4.** plants release this into the air

_____ **5.** plants reproduce by seeds or these

_____ **6.** it is inside the leaves of plants

_____ **7.** plants take this from the air

_____ **8.** the process by which plants and animals use and release gases

_____ **9.** gardening without soil

_____ **10.** they tell the age of a tree

a. carbon-dioxide cycle

b. seeds

c. annual rings

d. mold

e. hydroponics

f. carbon dioxide

g. photosynthesis

h. spores

i. oxygen

j. chlorophyll

Directions Answer each question about health.

11. How does a food pyramid help you to eat a healthy diet?

_____

_____

12. Why is it important to take care of the rain forests?

_____

_____

13. What is good first aid for a cut?

_____

_____

Life Science, p. 2

Directions Answer each question.

1. What are three features of living things?

_____

_____

_____

2. What is the difference between an extinct and an endangered population?

_____

_____

_____

3. Label the diagram with numbers 1–5 to order the steps of photosynthesis.

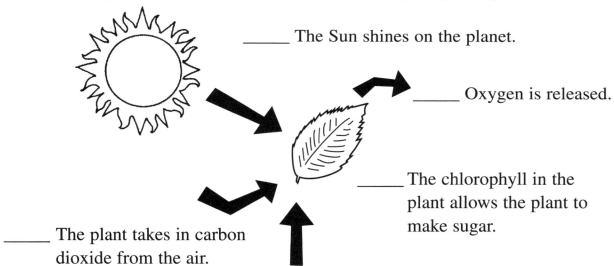

_____ The Sun shines on the planet.

_____ Oxygen is released.

_____ The chlorophyll in the plant allows the plant to make sugar.

_____ The plant takes in carbon dioxide from the air.

_____ Water enters the plant.

4. Number these drawings in the correct sequence to show the life cycle of the frog.

Physical Science

Directions Darken the circle for the correct answer.

1. Wedges are used to ____.

Ⓐ stick things together.
Ⓑ break things apart.
Ⓒ lift things.
Ⓓ lower things.

2. Deaf persons can tell if a stereo is on because ____.

Ⓐ they can hear the music.
Ⓑ they can feel the speakers.
Ⓒ they can see the sounds.
Ⓓ they see other people sing.

3. When all the colors of the spectrum are reflected, an object will look ____.

Ⓐ blue.   Ⓒ black.
Ⓑ red.   Ⓓ white.

4. The point where light beams meet after they pass through a lens is called the ____.

Ⓐ mirror.
Ⓑ prism.
Ⓒ reflection.
Ⓓ focal point.

5. A lever can be used to lift a heavy object by ____.

Ⓐ pushing down on one end of the bar.
Ⓑ pulling the object with the bar.
Ⓒ rolling the object with the bar.
Ⓓ putting the bar on top of the object.

6. A seesaw is ____.

Ⓐ a screw.
Ⓑ a wedge.
Ⓒ an inclined plane.
Ⓓ a lever.

7. A pulley is a wheel with ____.

Ⓐ a rope that does not move.
Ⓑ a lever attached to it.
Ⓒ an axle attached to it.
Ⓓ a rope that moves around it.

8. Music is made of vibrations ____.

Ⓐ that are loud.
Ⓑ that wind blows.
Ⓒ that move at the same rate.
Ⓓ with high pitches.

9. There is friction whenever ____.

Ⓐ two surfaces rub together.
Ⓑ an object is weighed.
Ⓒ an object does not move.
Ⓓ an object is lifted.

10. Bigger instruments make ____.

Ⓐ squeaky sounds.
Ⓑ sharp sounds.
Ⓒ high sounds.
Ⓓ low sounds.

Physical Science, p. 2

(Directions) Answer each question with a complete sentence.

1. Name three objects that use lenses.

_____

_____

_____

_____

2. How do sound waves travel?

_____

_____

_____

3. Why do your hands get warm when you rub them together?

_____

_____

_____

4. What is a spectrum?

_____

_____

_____

5. What two things happen to light as it gets farther from its source?

_____

_____

_____

Name _____   Date _____

Science Portfolio Assessment

Student's Name _____

Date _____

Goals	Evidence and Comments
1. Growth in understanding science concepts	_____ _____ _____ _____
2. Growth in using science processes	_____ _____ _____ _____
3. Growth in thinking critically	_____ _____ _____ _____
4. Growth in developing positive habits of mind and positive attitudes toward science	_____ _____ _____ _____

Social Studies Overall Assessment

(Directions) Darken the circle for the correct answer.

1. The governor of a state

  Ⓐ sees that the laws of the state are carried out.
  Ⓑ makes laws for the state.
  Ⓒ decides how people who break laws will be punished.
  Ⓓ is elected by state representatives.

2. In a democracy the people

  Ⓐ make choices about the government by voting.
  Ⓑ are not represented in government.
  Ⓒ have few responsibilities.
  Ⓓ have fewer rights than the leaders of the government.

3. The country's leading manufacturing state is

  Ⓐ Washington.   Ⓒ California.
  Ⓑ Oregon.   Ⓓ Hawaii.

4. What type of land is found in the Arctic Coastal Plane?

  Ⓐ rain forest   Ⓒ swamp
  Ⓑ desert   Ⓓ tundra

5. What was the Oklahoma Land Rush?

  Ⓐ people moving out of Oklahoma into Texas and New Mexico
  Ⓑ special areas in Oklahoma that were given to miners
  Ⓒ land in Oklahoma that was sold very cheaply
  Ⓓ people rushing into Oklahoma in search of free land

6. What effect do mountains have on the deserts in the Southwest region?

  Ⓐ The mountains prevent travel across the deserts.
  Ⓑ When the mountain snows melt, they bring drought to the deserts.
  Ⓒ The mountains stop winds from creating sand dunes.
  Ⓓ The mountains keep moist air from reaching the deserts.

7. A mission was

  Ⓐ a trading post.   Ⓒ a wildlife refuge.
  Ⓑ a Spanish settlement. Ⓓ a state park.

Go on to the next page.

Social Studies Overall Assessment, p. 2

Directions Darken the circle for the correct answer.

8. Because there were few trees, many settlers on the Great Plains built their homes out of

Ⓐ cement.

Ⓑ stone.

Ⓒ sod.

Ⓓ metal.

9. What is a wildlife refuge?

Ⓐ It is a region for hunting and fishing.

Ⓑ It is an area set aside to protect animals and other wildlife.

Ⓒ It is a place where animals can get better after an oil spill.

Ⓓ It is a place to protect people from wild animals.

10. The climate of the Pacific Northwest is especially good for growing

Ⓐ pineapples.   Ⓒ forests.

Ⓑ cactuses.   Ⓓ oranges.

11. Which of these statements about the United States *Constitution* is <u>not</u> true?

Ⓐ The *Constitution* is the "supreme law of the land."

Ⓑ The *Constitution* describes the rights that people in the United States have.

Ⓒ The *Constitution* is a written document.

Ⓓ The *Constitution* set up a federal government with four branches.

12. Which of these is a region that has an exact boundary and shares a government?

Ⓐ a city   Ⓒ a state

Ⓑ a county   Ⓓ all of these

13. Why do some people call the United States a "nation of immigrants"?

Ⓐ It has many visitors from around the world.

Ⓑ Few people are citizens.

Ⓒ People from around the world have come here to live.

Ⓓ The country's economy is based on world trade.

14. Which of these is <u>not</u> one of the Great Lakes?

Ⓐ Lake Huron   Ⓒ Lake Superior

Ⓑ Great Salt Lake   Ⓓ Lake Erie

Go on to the next page.

Name _____ Date _____

Social Studies Overall Assessment, p. 3

(Directions) Write the answer to each question in complete sentences.

1. What are the names of the seven continents?

_____

_____

2. Mass production and the assembly line were two important developments in American industry. Explain what they are and why they were important.

_____

_____

_____

_____

3. Explain two ways technology helps with communication today.

_____

_____

_____

4. Explain how railroads and rivers have been important in bringing people and products together.

_____

_____

_____

5. Explain how people have adapted to living in a desert environment.

_____

_____

_____

Name _____   Date _____

Reading Maps

(**Directions**) Darken the circle for the correct answer.

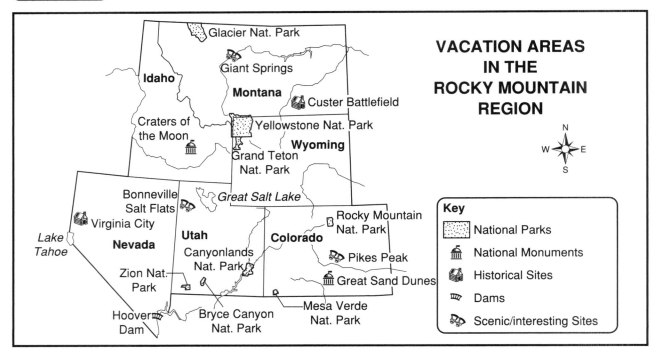

**VACATION AREAS
IN THE
ROCKY MOUNTAIN
REGION**

Key

- ▦ National Parks
- 🏛 National Monuments
- 🏠 Historical Sites
- ⚒ Dams
- 🚲 Scenic/interesting Sites

1. What scenic place is west of Utah's Great Salt Lake?

   Ⓐ Hoover Dam   Ⓑ Bonneville Salt Flats   Ⓒ Zion National Park

2. In what state is Yellowstone National Park?

   Ⓐ Colorado   Ⓑ Nevada   Ⓒ Wyoming

3. In what state is Craters of the Moon National Monument?

   Ⓐ Nevada   Ⓑ Colorado   Ⓒ Idaho

4. What is the name of the historical site in Montana?

   Ⓐ Giant Springs   Ⓑ Custer Battlefield   Ⓒ Glacier National Park

5. What national park is located west of Bryce Canyon National Park?

   Ⓐ Zion National Park   Ⓑ Mesa Verde National Park   Ⓒ Hoover Dam

Name _____ Date _____

Reading Maps

(**Directions**) Read the questions. Use the map to find the answers. Write your answers.

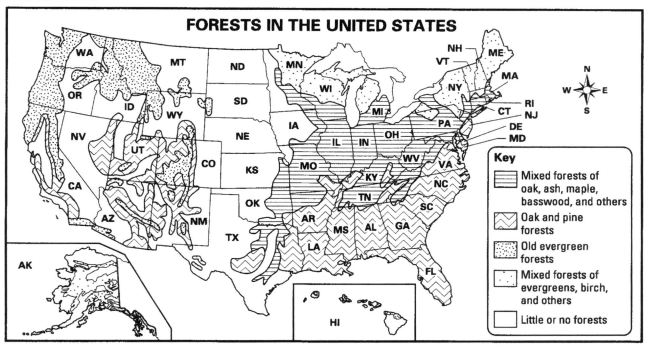

FORESTS IN THE UNITED STATES

Key
- Mixed forests of oak, ash, maple, basswood, and others
- Oak and pine forests
- Old evergreen forests
- Mixed forests of evergreens, birch, and others
- Little or no forests

1. Write the name of a state in which you would find old evergreen forests.

_____

2. What kind of forest grows in the northeast part of the United States?

_____

3. Find the state where you live. What kind of trees or forests grow in your state?

_____

4. Does your state have oak or pine forests?

_____

5. Name a state that has no forests of any kind.

_____

Reading Time Lines

(**Directions**) Use the time line to answer the questions.

Important Events in U.S. History

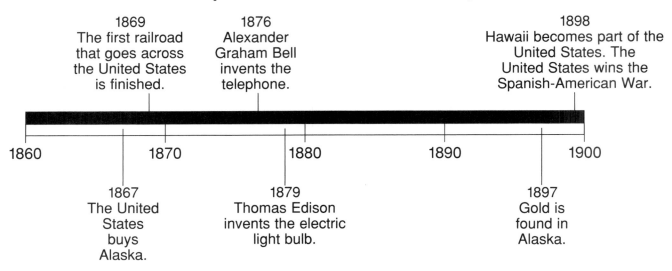

1. Which event happened first: the invention of the electric light bulb or telephone?

_____

2. Which event occurred in 1897?

_____

3. What event happened in 1867?

_____

4. World War II was fought during the 1940s. Would it appear on this time line?

_____

5. When was the trancontinental railroad completed?

_____

6. What year did the U.S. win the Spanish-American War?

_____

Skills Assessments, Grade 4
Answer Key

Page 5
1. C
2. B
3. A
4. C
5. B
6. A
7. C
8. C
9. B

Page 6
10. D
11. C
12. D
13. D

Page 7
1. B
2. D
3. C
4. A
5. C
6. B
7. D
8. D
9. B
10. B

Page 8
1. A
2. B
3. C
4. B
5. A
6. A
7. B
8. C
9. B
10. A

Page 9
1. A
2. B
3. C
4. B
5. C
6. D
7. A
8. B
9. C
10. A
11. B
12. B
13. A
14. D
15. C

Page 10
1. C
2. C
3. B
4. C
5. A
6. A
7. C
8. A
9. A
10. B
11. C
12. C
13. C
14. C

Page 11
1. B
2. A
3. B
4. A
5. D
6. B
7. D
8. B
9. C
10. B
11. D
12. A

Page 12
1. A
2. D
3. B
4. C
5. C
6. B
7. C
8. B
9. D
10. C

Page 13
1. D
2. A
3. C
4. B
5. C
6. C
7. B
8. A
9. A
10. C

Page 14
1. A
2. A
3. C
4. D
5. C
6. A
7. A
8. B
9. D
10. B

Page 15
1. A
2. B
3. B
4. C
5. D
6. B
7. C
8. B
9. D
10. B

Page 16
1. D
2. B
3. C
4. D
5. B
6. B
7. A
8. D
9. B
10. B

Page 17
1. D
2. A
3. B
4. A
5. B
6. D
7. C
8. B
9. B
10. D

Page 18
1. B
2. A
3. B
4. C
5. D
6. D

Page 19
1. B
2. A
3. A
4. A
5. D
6. D

Page 20
1. A
2. D
3. D
4. C
5. A

Page 21
1. A
2. D
3. B
4. B

Page 22
1. A
2. D
3. C

Page 23
1. C
2. C
3. B
4. C

Page 25
1. C
2. A
3. C
4. A
5. D
6. B
7. C
8. A

Page 27
1. Sylvia loved the little bear because Lin made it just for her.
2. Sylvia was a kind and generous girl.
3. Sylvia's parents told her to stop because she could have been hurt in the fire.
4. Lin gave Sylvia the bear because she wanted to repay Sylvia's kindness.
5. Sylvia found the bear in the mail.

Page 29
1. C
2. A
3. B
4. D
5. C

Page 31
1. *Reaction* means a response to something.
2. Coach Penn shook his head because the team was not playing together.
3. The Panthers was a basketball team.
4. The Panthers played the Bulldogs on Friday.
5. Every player contributed to the victory.

Page 34
1. A
2. C
3. A
4. B
5. B
6. C
7. B
8. A
9. C
10. A

Page 37
1. Magellan found a route that led all the way around the world. or Magellan tried to reach the Spice Islands by sailing west.
2. King Charles V ruled Spain.
3. It took Magellan two months to cross the Atlantic Ocean.

Page 37 con't.
4. *Pacific* means the peaceful sea.
5. The Pacific is over 11,000 miles wide.

Pages 38–39
1. B
2. A
3. D
4. B
5. B
6. B
7. D
8. title page
9. table of contents
10. glossary
11. index
12. A
13. B
14. A
15. A
16. A
17. A
18. B
19. B
20. B

Page 40
1. A
2. B
3. A
4. C
5. D
6. C
7. A
8. C
9. D
10. D

Page 41
1. A
2. A
3. D
4. D
5. A
6. D
7. A
8. C
9. B
10. A

Page 42
1. A
2. C
3. A
4. D
5. A
6. B
7. D
8. A
9. C
10. C

Page 43
1. C
2. D
3. A
4. B
5. B
6. B
7. D
8. A
9. A
10. A

Page 44
1. Mrs. Smith; job
2. picnic; family
3. family; picnic
4. event; year
5. Margie; hamburgers
6. Mrs. Smith; Riverview Park
7. park; Mississippi River
8. place
9. person
10. place
11. thing
12. place
13. person
14. person
15. place

Page 45
1. D
2. C
3. B
4. C
5. B
6. C
7. D
8. A
9. A
10. C

Page 46
1. B
2. A
3. C
4. D
5. A
6. C
7. D
8. A
9. A
10. A

Page 47
1. C
2. D
3. C
4. A
5. C
6. C
7. A
8. C
9. C
10. D

Page 48
1. B
2. B
3. B
4. C
5. B
6. C
7. B
8. A
9. C
10. B

Page 49
1. B
2. A
3. D
4. A
5. A
6. A

Page 50
1. D
2. C
3. A
4. B
5. D
6. B
7. A
8. A
9. C
10. A

Page 51
1. C
2. D
3. B
4. C
5. A
6. B
7. C
8. C
9. B
10. B

Page 53
1. A
2. D
3. C
4. B
5. A
6. C
7. B
8. B
9. B
10. D

Page 54
1. A Number of Stories
2. 42
3. Brandywine Arts, Inc.
4. Lisa Newton
5. Adding It Up
6. double
7. 25–33, 62
8. 58–60, 119
9. A solution to an arithmetic problem
10. four

Page 55
1. lake/lawn
2. lake
3. lamp
4. lap
5. last
6. late
7. lawn
8. pack/pass
9. pack
10. pad
11. page
12. palm
13. pan
14. pass
15. three
16. detector
17. club/detector
18. no

Page 56
1. B
2. D
3. B
4. D
5. A
6. C
7. B
8. D

Page 57
1. They found bricks made by Grandpa Weaver.
2. He is 75. He is a schoolteacher. He is married. He built a patio.
3. They were schoolteachers for 40 years.
4. Answers will vary. Be sure the paragraph has a main idea and supporting details.

Page 58
1. Kangaroos are not the only unusual animals that are native to Australia.
2. Responses will vary. Be sure each sentence has a detail.
3. grass, flowers, insects, and almost anything else
4. Answers will vary. Be sure the paragraph has a main idea and supporting details.

Answer Key, p. 2

Page 59
1. Musical chairs is a good game to play with a group of friends.
2. It tells how to decide who wins.
3. It names the game.
4. It gives the materials needed to play.
5. They tell how to play the game.
6. Answers will vary. A how-to paragraph has a topic sentence, has details that tell what materials are needed, uses time order words, and gives directions in order.

Page 60
1. Every student should be required to read *Johnny Tremain*.
2. In the first sentence or the topic sentence.
3. Students can learn about an important time in American History by reading this book.
4. a. F
   b. O
   c. O
   d. F
   e. F
5. Answers will vary.

Page 61
1. B
2. C
3. D
4. B
5. A
6. A
7. D
8. B
9. B
10. C

Page 62
11. C
12. C
13. B
14. A
15. B
16. A
17. 7:45 AM
18. 24, 39, 63, 102

Page 63
1. A
2. C
3. C
4. C
5. D
6. C
7. C
8. A
9. D
10. D

Page 64
1. C
2. D
3. C
4. B
5. B
6. D
7. B
8. A
9. A
10. C

Page 65
1. D
2. B
3. B
4. A
5. C
6. B
7. B
8. A
9. A
10. D

Page 66
1. A
2. C
3. B
4. A
5. D
6. C
7. C
8. D
9. B
10. B

Page 67
1. D
2. C
3. A
4. C
5. A
6. C
7. B
8. C
9. B
10. D

Page 68
1. D
2. D
3. A
4. C
5. A
6. B
7. A
8. B
9. A
10. D

Page 69
1. C
2. B
3. B
4. C
5. D
6. D
7. B
8. C
9. A
10. B

Page 70
1. B
2. D
3. A
4. A
5. B
6. A
7. B
8. A
9. D
10. A

Page 71
1. dog
2. 16
3. 36
4. 12 in 36, 1 in 3, or 1/3, or 12/36
5. B
6. B
7. C

Page 72
1. 8, 13, 21, 34
2. 16, 26, 42, 68
3. 48, 96, 192
4. 80, 160, 320
5. C
6. A
7. B
8. A
9. C
10. B

Page 73
1. B
2. ↓
3. ⬡
4. ⊠
5. ▢
6. ▭

Page 74
1. >
2. <
3. $ 0.55
4. A
5. D
6. A
7. C

Page 75
1. May 6
2. May 14
3. 16 hours
4. months
5. minutes
6. minutes
7. 5 hours
8. 35 minutes

Page 76
1. a. 78°F
   b. 3°C
2. a. 3 minutes
   b. 15 minutes
   c. 2 seconds
3. B
4. B
5. A
6. C
7. A
8. C

Page 77
1. B
2. B
3. C
4. B
5. A
6. B
7. D
8. B
9. C
10. C

Page 78
1. B
2. B
3. C
4. C
5. A
6. A
7. A
8. A
9. D
10. B

Page 79
1. D
2. B
3. C
4. B
5. B
6. D
7. A
8. B

Page 80
1. $0.65
2. 97.3
3. $3.74
4. 1/4 white
5. 2/10 or 1/5 gray
6. 3 1/3 yards
7. 2 packages for $9.04
8. 1 1/12

Page 81
1. A
2. D
3. B
4. C
5. C
6. A
7. C
8. B
9. B
10. B

Page 82
1. B
2. A
3. C
4. A
5. C
6. A
7. B
8. D
9. A
10. A

Page 83
1. Lists will vary.
2. Answers will vary. Possible responses: Hurricanes form over tropical oceans, but tornadoes do not need an ocean to form. The centers of hurricanes are much stronger than the centers of tornadoes. Hurricanes can cause more damage than tornadoes.
3. Nitrogen makes up the largest part of air.
4. Answers will vary. Possible responses: to see trends in how weather is changing; to predict what the weather will be like in a few days; to prepare for weather events that can be predicted; so people will know how to dress or what activities to plan.
5. The Moon moves between the Earth and the Sun, blocking the sunlight.

Page 84
1. g
2. d
3. b
4. i
5. h
6. j
7. f
8. a
9. e
10. c
(Wording of the answers may vary.)
11. The food pyramid gives the amount of each type of food you need to eat to have a balanced diet.
12. Rain forests provide foods that cannot be found elsewhere. They provide medicinal plants, and they provide a home for people and animals.
13. A cut should be washed and covered with a clean bandage.

Page 85
(Wording of the answers will vary.)
1. a. Living things can reproduce.
   b. Living things grow and change.
   c. Living things need food and water for energy.
2. An extinct population no longer exists, while an endangered population is in danger of becoming extinct.
3. 1. Sun shines on the plant.
   2. The plant takes in carbon dioxide from the air.
   3. Water enters the plant.
   4. The chlorophyll in the plant allows the plant to make sugar.
   5. Oxygen is released.
4. 2, 1, 4, 3

Page 86
1. B
2. B
3. D
4. D
5. A
6. D
7. D
8. C
9. A
10. D

Page 87
1. Answers will vary. Possible answers: Telescopes, microscopes, eyeglasses, magnifying glasses, and cameras use lenses.
2. Sound waves move out in all directions. As they move out, they bump into air molecules and other objects, causing them to move, too.
3. Rubbing causes friction and friction causes heat.
4. A spectrum is seven colors that make up light.
5. Light spreads out and dims as it moves away from the light source.

Page 89
1. A
2. A
3. C
4. D
5. D
6. D
7. B

Page 90
8. C
9. B
10. C
11. D
12. D
13. C
14. B

Page 91
1. The seven continents are North America, South America, Europe, Asia, Africa, Australia, and Antarctica.
2. Answers will vary. Possible response: Mass production means making many things that are all alike. An assembly line is a line of workers along which a product moves as it is put together one step at a time. These developments helped industries make products faster and more cheaply so that more people could afford to buy them.
3. Answers will vary. Responses should include the ideas that technology makes communications faster, easier, and cheaper.
4. Answers will vary. Both railroads and rivers are important to transportation. Railroads take products from the farms to the cities. They also take products from the cities to the farms. Rivers also take products from one area of the country to another. Rivers take natural resources to factories, and they link inland regions with the oceans.
5. Answers will vary. Possible responses: People have adapted to living in a desert environment by building with adobe, building aqueducts, building reservoirs, using air conditioning, using solar energy, and using irrigation.

Page 92
1. B
2. C
3. C
4. B
5. A

Page 93
1. Answers will vary. Some possible answers: Washington, Montana, Idaho, Oregon, California, Colorado, Wyoming, New Mexico
2. Mixed forests of evergreens, birch and others.
3. Answers will vary
4. Answers will vary
5. Answers will vary. Possible answers: North Dakota or Nebraska

Page 94
1. telephone
2. Gold discovered in Alaska
3. U.S. buys Alaska
4. No
5. 1869
6. 1898